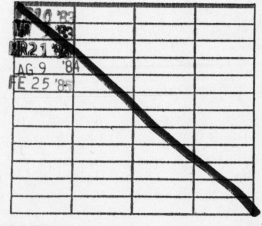

Perspectives on Gifted and Talented Education

GIFTED YOUNG CHILDREN

Wendy Conklin Roedell
Nancy Ewald Jackson
Halbert B. Robinson
Child Development Research Group
University of Washington

Perspectives on Gifted and Talented Education

Abraham J. Tannenbaum
Director

Elizabeth Neuman
Editor

Gifted and Talented Project
Teachers College, Columbia University

Teachers College, Columbia University
New York and London   1980

This work was developed under a contract with the U.S. Office of
Education, Department of Health, Education, and Welfare. However, the
content does not necessarily reflect the position or policy of that Agency,
and no official endorsement of these materials should be inferred.

Library of Congress Cataloging in Publication Data

Roedell, Wendy Conklin, 1943–
   Gifted young children.

   (Perspectives on gifted and talented education)
   Bibliography: p.
   Includes index.
   1. Gifted children—Education. I. Jackson,
Nancy Ewald, joint author. II. Robinson,
Halbert B., joint author. III. Title.
IV. Series.
LC3993.R62   371.95   80-10707
ISBN 0-8077-2587-0

Design by Romeo Enriquez

8 7 6 5 4 3 2 1 80 81 82 83 84 85 86 87
Printed in the U.S.A.

CONTENTS

TABLES

FOREWORD

GIFTED CHILDREN WHO draw attention to themselves—and not all do—through their precocity are constantly in the public eye, sometimes as stars, sometimes as sties. They cannot be ignored, but they can be neglected. Professionals and laymen alike have often reacted ambivalently to these children, appreciating their special qualities while doubting their right to special educational enrichment on the grounds that it smacks of elitism. There are educators who believe that the gifted can make it on their own without extra help and regard differentiated programs for such children as luxuries that are welcome when they are affordable and quickly disposable when they are not. What counts most according to this point of view is the "golden mean," or normalcy, as reflected in the normal curve of ability and performance. Whoever fails to measure up to the golden mean has a right to every kind of compensatory assistance; whoever exceeds levels of functioning that are normal or average for most children may receive applause but no extra attention. Rarely is thought given to the possibility that democratic education means stretching each child's mind to its own outer limits without injury to mental or physical health.

Fortunately growing interest in the gifted at school is helping sharpen public concern for the individualities of *all* children. Differentiated education is beginning to replace procrustean education, and fewer people are making a fetish of averageness in the normal curve. Yet, this new awareness that "sameness" and "equality" are *not* synonymous terms when they refer to educational opportunity has not always led to a clear understanding of existing knowledge in the field. A great many myths have masqueraded as truisms, and they tend to be reinforced rather than exploded in some of the awareness rallies, lectures, and workshops on behalf of gifted children. Even the professional literature has been affected by unsubstantiated claims about the nature and nurture of giftedness and by rhetoric that appeals more to the emotions than to reason.

It is time that some clearer impressions were recorded about the "state of the art" in understanding and educating the gifted in order to counterbalance some of the distortions, wishful thinking, overblown claims, and misdirected evangelism that has plagued the field. The intention of this Teachers College series of original monographs is to contribute to that kind of corrective. It has grown out of a federally supported contract to develop information products on key topics pertaining to the gifted and to bring them to the attention of the general public, including laymen and professionals. The authors have devoted considerable care to the content of their statements and the consequent impact on readers. Each writer is eminently qualified to make a balanced, meaningful contribution that avoids simply paraphrasing what others have said earlier. The aim is to inform through cogent presentations that can be appreciated by the widest possible audience ranging from those who want to be initiated to those who seek new insights into the field of educating the gifted.

Abraham J. Tannenbaum
Teachers College, Columbia University

PREFACE

In writing this monograph, the authors have reviewed and synthesized most of what is known about the intellectual and social development of gifted young children. While the volume focuses on gifted children of preschool age, much of the material is also relevant for understanding gifted children in the early elementary years. Our aim is to present a scholarly, yet practical guide for those working with gifted young children on a day-to-day basis, particularly those engaged in identifying such children and planning programs to match their special gifts and talents.

We also hope that this synthesis of current knowledge will serve as a springboard for the research needed to increase our understanding of young children's skills.

Much of the information in this review was generated by the Child Development Research Group of Seattle, which began a long-term study of children with advanced intellectual abilities in the fall of 1974, a study that will continue until the children, now of preschool age, reach adulthood. Halbert B. Robinson is the study's principal investigator; Nancy E. Jackson and Wendy C. Roedell are associate investigators. At present, the longitudinal study focuses on more than 300 children nominated by their parents as demonstrating some advanced intellectual ability before the age of five. Within the group are 53 children whose abilities are in the extraordinary range—four standard deviations above the mean for their age group and or equal to the performance of average children twice their chronological age. The group also includes children who have not demonstrated unusually advanced abilities on any psychometric test, but who are considered to be "at risk" for extraordinary precocity on the basis of their parents' judgment.

In addition to the longitudinal study, the Seattle project sponsors several programs designed to facilitate the education of intellectually advanced children. The Diagnostic and Counseling Service provides families of intellectually advanced children with a comprehensive assessment of their child's abilities and counseling regarding educational placement and personal and social development. The Child Development Preschool serves young children with advanced intellectual skills. The Early Entrance Program is a program of early admission to the University of Washington for qualified junior high school students. The Seattle project has also been instrumental in the development of the Individual Progress Program, a program for academically talented students currently operated by the Seattle public school system in collaboration with the project staff. Taken together, these programs provide the framework for a coordinated preschool-through-university educational system for children with extraordinarily advanced intellectual or academic skills.

The Seattle project has been supported by grants from the Spencer, Ford, and

Medina Foundations and from the U.S. Office of Education. The material collected in this volume was prepared under a subcontract from Teachers College, Columbia University. We wish to thank Teachers College, Columbia University and our contract officer, Elizabeth Neuman, for their support of this work.

While we all collaborated on all parts of this monograph, different individuals had primary responsibility for different chapters. Principal authorship is indicated in footnotes to each chapter.

We are grateful for the painstaking efforts of Wendy Hutchins-Cook. She scoured the library for relevant materials, wrote summary notes on countless articles, and carefully prepared the bibliography. Thanks are also due to Marti Sivertson and Marilyn Moore for their patience and skill in typing numerous drafts of the manuscript.

Wendy Conklin Roedell
Nancy Ewald Jackson
Halbert B. Robinson

1

CONCERNING
THE NATURE
OF GIFTEDNESS

THE IDEA OF giftedness is a complex one; its interpretation has changed through the years. Even today it has different meanings for different people. Our first task, therefore, is to clarify what we mean by the concept of giftedness. Then we will describe young gifted children, propose ways to identify them, and explore the types of educational programs that have been made available for them.

DEFINITIONS OF GIFTEDNESS

Definitions of giftedness vary according to the values of a given society. In a primitive but stable society, it may be the most successful hunter or the most compelling storyteller whose abilities are accorded highest value. In an advanced and complex society, like ours, superiority in abstract reasoning is usually recognized as an important gift. We also regard the talents of the Olympic gold-medal athlete, the celebrated musician, and the eminent statesman with respect, along with winners of Nobel Prizes for the sciences and literature. Neither our own society nor any other, however, regards everything that individuals do exceptionally well as evidence of giftedness.

Our definition of giftedness has most often involved professional eminence or recognized achievement. It is rarely equated with outstanding performance on an arbitrary measure, such as an intelligence test, but rather with outstanding performance in the real world. It is the product a person produces —a scientific discovery, a political victory, a poem of lyric beauty, a philosophical treatise—that reveals the gifted adult. Persons of high ability whose "light is hidden under a bushel" are not likely to be regarded as gifted. Studies of gifted adults, such as those of Cox (1926) and McCurdy (1957), have tended to set very high standards indeed, defining giftedness against not only contemporary but historical tests. The major criterion in these studies has shifted subtly to "greatness" rather than "giftedness."

Gifted children, however, lack these touchstones of adult success, having had less opportunity to realize the full extent of their gifts. The goal in identifying

---

The principal author of this chapter is Halbert B. Robinson.

gifted children is to recognize talent so that it can be nurtured. Definitions of giftedness in children, therefore, have tended to be in terms of test performance. In the literature about children, giftedness is most often assumed to be a form of intellectual precocity, usually defined as a high score on a test of general intelligence. The criteria for high performance differ from study to study. Most studies specify a minimum IQ of 120 to 140, but in many instances the threshold of giftedness has been defined as high as 160 or even 180.

Recently the definition of giftedness in children has been broadened. According to the U.S. Commissioner of Education (1972) it is recommended that gifted children be identified not only by measures of intellectual ability and scholastic aptitude, but also by indices of creativity, leadership, talent in the visual and performing arts, and psychomotor ability.

Proposing multiple criteria, however, does not solve the controversy about the nature of giftedness. Is giftedness a unitary phenomenon, that is, composed of elements that are simply different ways of getting at what is, on an underlying level, an all purpose unitary trait? Or is giftedness multifactorial, that is, composed of distinct factors that are relatively independent?

If one considers giftedness to be a unitary trait, one would expect a great deal of congruence in talents, while still using multiple criteria to discover giftedness. The assumption is that high ability can be channeled into a number of achievement areas. A child with exceptional reading skills, for example, should also exhibit a capacity for rapid learning in reasoning and arithmetic. In this sense, the multiple criteria used to define giftedness are much like blind men describing an elephant, each revealing a different part of a single phenomenon, the gifted child. This assumption that multiple indices represent different facets of a singular underlying ability provides the basis for programming in some educational systems (Pennsylvania Department of Education, 1973). Thus, some programs for the gifted, while designed to admit children on the basis of several different kinds of achievement, treat them similarly once enrolled. It is expected that all gifted children, whether identified on the basis of leadership skill, artistic ability, or mathematical reasoning skills, will profit from working together in a single program, with some allowance made for their individual differences.

If, however, one considers giftedness to be composed of a variety of talents and skills, all varying more or less independently, one would not expect the same congruence of abilities. Consider the three Rs of education—reading, writing, and arithmetic. If skills in these three academic areas vary independently, an unusually high level of ability in one area may not necessarily coexist with similarly high levels of ability in the other areas. One might look for children who are gifted in reading, in writing, or in arithmetic and not expect that these would necessarily be the same children. Likewise, one would not expect children with unusual artistic talent to be equally able in academic subject areas. Programs based on this multifactor concept of giftedness are similarly multifaceted. Mathematically gifted children require a program of a different nature than verbally, interpersonally, or artistically gifted children. Different provisions are needed to foster the unique talents of each of these types of children. Again, the definition of giftedness has immediate and compelling consequences for educational programming.

Although giftedness may take many different forms, most of the literature concerning gifted children defines giftedness in terms of superior intellectual ability, and much of the literature reviewed here is devoted to ways of measuring and interpreting intellectual skills. But limiting the definition of giftedness to intelligence does not eliminate the problem of whether giftedness can be considered a unitary trait. In fact, there is continuing debate as to whether intelligence itself is a single entity. It is appropriate, therefore, to pause and reflect on the meaning of the term "intelligence."

DEFINITIONS OF INTELLIGENCE

Surely prehistoric human beings were aware that some of their fellows were cleverer than others, better problem-solvers, better able to make sense of a puzzling or frightening situation, more likely to invent an effective tool or to design a better shelter or a more potent weapon, better able to use language and other symbols to express and record ideas.

There is little doubt that people have long noted and cared about variations in talents and skills. Yet from the time of the Greeks onward, no single definition of intelligence appears to have ever satisfied everyone. Indeed, there are few concepts that have remained as confused and controversial as this one. In general, it might be said, the term refers to one's ability to acquire knowledge and to use it in solving new and complex problems. But even this simple definition has aroused considerable disagreement.

One of the controversies revolves around the question of the organization of abilities. This stems from the same argument of whether intelligence should be considered a unitary trait, a characteristic that is general, pervasive, and all-of-a-piece, or should it be considered a summation of separate, distinct abilities that vary more or less independently? Proponents of the unitary point of view tend to talk about a *general* factor (sometimes called *g-factor* after the work of Charles Spearman, a noted English psychologist and statistician). They emphasize the commonalities or correlations that appear in individuals' performances over a broad range of tasks used to measure cognitive abilities. They think of a fundamental, unitary attribute involved to some extent in all human endeavors, but certainly in those requiring some degree of problem-solving. They tend to favor and to develop closely related measures of a single characteristic, intelligence.

Opposed to this view are those who maintain that intelligence is not composed of a single factor but, in fact, consists of a large number of elementary abilities, or *specific factors,* associated with human abilities. One theorist, E.L. Thorndike (1921), felt the number of such abilities corresponded with the number and kinds of neural connections in the brain. Another, J. P. Guilford (1967) listed some 120 specific abilities and suggested that the abilities that appear to be included in the notion of intelligence are independent of one another; thus, high or low ability in one area is thought to have little or no relation to high or low ability in other areas.

Not surprisingly, many psychologists take a compromise view, maintaining that mental abilities cannot be described adequately with a single factor, but that the very large number of specific factors proposed by Thorndike, Guilford, and others is both unwieldy and unnecessary. They see various specific factors coalescing into *group factors,* limited in number but still revealing qualitative differences among people. The most familiar distinction is between verbal and performance ability areas as defined by David Wechsler (1974). Others, analyzing tests given to various population groups, have suggested, for example, such components of intelligence as memory, spatial reasoning, and verbal capacity.

It is important to point out that these theoretical disputes have had little effect on the use of intelligence tests. While some tests, such as the Stanford-Binet Intelligence Scale, may be biased in favor of discovering and measuring a *g-factor* and others, such as the Wechsler tests, may be slanted toward *group factors,* the IQ derived from the Stanford-Binet and the Full-Scale IQ derived from the Wechsler tests are highly comparable. Indeed, for most psychologists and educators, theoretical quarrels have largely been put aside, while the practical utility of the intelligence tests has been given prominence. The test scores have been shown to be effective (though far from perfect) predictors of achievement in school subjects that demand complex verbal skills and in other situations that make similar demands. There has emerged a strong tendency, in fact, to equate intelligence with performance on the psychological tests designed to measure it —that is, to equate intelligence and IQ—and to ignore the controversies and uncertainties about the nature of the concept.

AGE AND INTELLIGENCE

Age plays an important role in current understanding of intelligence. The way that intelligence is organized in adults, for example, may not be the same in children. Traditionally it has been thought that young children are not as differentiated in their abilities as are older children. Infants and preschoolers are, it has been believed, more likely to show the same level of ability in one area as another, while older children and adults show clearer differences in the levels of their various capacities. To anticipate some of the material that will be discussed later, our studies of exceptionally precocious children at the University of Washington suggest that even in children as young as two years of age, different patterns of ability can be described. In other words, with exceptionally precocious children, at least, it appears that different kinds of talent do play a role from a very early age. We find some who are reading at second grade level or above by age two, some who perform unusually well on tasks requiring spatial ability, some who are extraordinarily facile with numbers, and some whose memory abilities are phenomenal. These tend to be *different* children although, to be sure, there are some relationships among their scores. Further, there are some children who obtain very high scores on tests of intelligence such as the Stanford-Binet, a test that taps several areas of functioning. These high-scoring children are not always equally outstanding readers, spatial reasoners, or memorizers. In other words, it seems clear that we must attend to independent factors in intelligence even in very young gifted children. Whether the same holds true of children with lesser abilities remains to be discovered.

Age enters the picture of intelligence in a second way as well. The first intelligence tests, devised by Binet at the turn of the century in Paris, were age scales. Children's performance was evaluated according to the average age of those who gave similar responses. Soon it became apparent that intelligence could be thought of as the "mental age" a child attained on a test in relation to the child's chronological age. The resulting ratio indicated *rate* of development, or the speed with which new skills and abilities were emerging, in relationship to the averages for all children. While we no longer use age in precisely the same way in calculating IQs, the *rate* notion still has value. Preschool children who are "only" two to four years advanced in mental performance are, then, very advanced indeed. Their intellectual development can be considered to be proceeding at double the rate at which development proceeds in average children.

CONCERN FOR GIFTED CHILDREN

In the United States interest in gifted children has waxed and waned over the years. One era of interest occurred during the 1920s and 1930s, a period when tests of intelligence were being developed. It was thought then that children exhibited stable, genetically-determined rates of intellectual growth that should be discovered as early as possible. Interest in giftedness ebbed considerably following that era but was reawakened in the post-Sputnik period of the late 1950s, when there was a flurry of activity in science education and a search for talented young people to provide technical and scientific leadership. The country's interest, however, soon became preoccupied with the problems of the poor and the undereducated, and priority was given to providing equal opportunity for entire segments of society that had suffered the ills of discrimination and poverty.

There are, however, many signs today of another reawakening of attention to the identification and nurturance of highly talented children who can be identified in all segments of society. We are beginning to recognize the needs of these children for special experiences that are commensurate with their abilities. We are also beginning to recognize society's own needs for the unusual contributions of which they are potentially capable.

For the past 30 years, we have not done well by such children. Many highly talented youngsters have become discouraged and have "dropped out" or "opted out" of productive involvement, at great cost to themselves and to society as a whole. Early identification and programming for children with special talents can reduce this tragic loss. This monograph reviews the sum of our knowledge about the very young gifted child. It is hoped that this review will contribute to society's efforts to nurture the gifts of the very young.

2

CHARACTERISTICS OF GIFTED YOUNG CHILDREN

Pᴿᴏᴹɪɴᴇɴᴛ ɪɴ ᴛʜᴇ literature concerning gifted children are checklists of characteristics that are said to distinguish them from other children (see, e.g., Abraham, 1976; Barbe, 1956; Hildreth, 1938). The gifted are said to be superior in almost all respects. A typical checklist (Abraham, 1976), for example, indicates that gifted children learn to walk and talk at earlier ages than average children. They are larger, stronger, and healthier than average children. They have longer attention spans, are better adjusted, more trustworthy, and have a better sense of humor. Other descriptions indicate that gifted children are persistent in the face of difficulty, happy, busy, independent, and active (Hildreth, 1938). They are dominant, forceful, independent, and competitive (Gallagher, 1975); they reject conformity, prize independence, and possess high social values and ideals (Newland, 1976).

Most of these descriptions of the overall superiority of gifted children are derived from studies that have compared groups of gifted children, usually identified by a single intelligence test score, with various groups from the general population. The monumental study of Lewis Terman and his associates (Burks, Jensen, & Terman, 1930; Oden, 1968; 1959) set the stage for this type of research. Terman and his colleagues did, in fact, find that comparisons of gifted and average groups on many physical and social characteristics yielded slight mean differences in favor of the gifted group. However, in Terman's and most other similar studies the mean differences favoring the gifted group have tended to be small and have sometimes disappeared when the comparison group was appropriately matched for variables such as social class.

Reviewers looking for simple descriptions of the gifted child have ignored Terman's own warnings that gifted children show wide variability with respect to every trait measured. Terman and Oden (1947) pointed out that the individuals in their sample did not fall into a single or easily described pattern. Every type of personality defect, social maladjustment, behavior problem, and physical frailty was represented in the gifted group. In a study of gifted children in primary schools in England, Ogilvie (1973) found that gifted children differ so much among them-

---

The principal author of this chapter is Wendy Conklin Roedell.

selves that he was forced to conclude that "any list of traits can only be misleading." Case studies of gifted children have strongly supported this conclusion (Hauck & Freehill, 1972; Hildreth, 1954). Professionals seldom agree as to what set of characteristics should be used to typify the gifted child. When one group of teachers and guidance counselors was asked to describe the essential characteristics of gifted children, they described a wide range of traits, including many which were contradictory, such as both introvertive and extrovertive characteristics (Chen & Goon, 1976).

It is obvious, of course, that the characteristics chosen to describe gifted children will vary depending on the definition of giftedness employed. It makes sense, perhaps, to discuss the physical characteristics of gifted children if one is trying to describe children gifted in the psychomotor realm. Likewise, discussion of social characteristics may be appropriate when considering children with leadership ability. Most researchers, however, have defined giftedness as a high score on a standard measure of intelligence and have then attempted to identify nonintellective characteristics that distinguish these high-scoring children from children with average scores. Many of these studies suffer from biases in sample selection, which confound the findings. In Terman's study, for example, most children in the sample were selected by teacher nomination. Schools in "good" neighborhoods were canvassed more thoroughly than schools in poorer neighborhoods since the likelihood of finding bright children in higher socioeconomic populations seemed greater. When such children's physical characteristics are compared with national norms, the mean differences between groups may be attributed as much to socioeconomic status as to IQ differences. Likewise, the children originally nominated by teachers as good prospects for having a high IQ were likely to be those who were well adjusted in school. They were consequently more likely to show a positive constellation of social and personality characteristics than were equally bright students not nominated by their teachers and so not included in the sample.

In the remaining sections of this chapter, the family backgrounds of gifted children, their physical characteristics, their early development, their social and emotional development, and their patterns of intellectual ability will be considered in turn. Since research focusing on preschool-aged children is scarce, relevant studies of older children will also be reviewed.

FAMILY BACKGROUND

Several studies have found that many children with high IQ scores come from upper and middle socioeconomic backgrounds and have well-educated parents who were born in the United States (Barbe, 1956; Cattell, 1915; Hitchfield, 1973; Hollingworth, 1942; Parkyn, 1948; Sheldon, 1954; Terman & Oden, 1947). In one study, it was found that mothers of gifted children tend to be well-educated, to have few children, and to be employed outside the home

(Groth, 1975). Mothers of highly gifted children surveyed in another study tended to dislike housework (Sheldon, 1954). The sample of preschool-aged children with advanced intellectual abilities identified by the Seattle project tend also to come from middle- and upper middle-class families (Robinson, Jackson, & Roedell, 1977).

On the other hand, several studies indicate that lower income and minority group populations may also yield large numbers of children in all areas (Chen & Goon, 1976; Jenkins, 1943). Some of the issues involved in identifying gifted children from culturally different populations are discussed in Chapter 3. It is quite possible that children from low income and minority backgrounds have appeared less frequently in studies of gifted children simply because their families are less likely to choose to participate in research. Certainly there is abundant evidence that gifted children can be identified in all cultural and economic groups.

Several studies have indicated that parents' education is correlated with various measures of intellectual ability in their young children. In a recent study (Willerman & Fiedler, 1977) of 114 children who had Binet IQs of 140 or above at age four, it was found that parent education was correlated with both IQ and achievement scores for boys, but only with achievement scores for girls. When the children were retested at age seven, the correlation of mother's education with son's IQ, and of both parents' education with some of the achievement measures for both sexes remained significant. It was noted that children whose IQs dropped between the ages of four and seven had less well-educated parents than children whose IQs remained high. In addition, boys whose IQs dropped came from larger families; girls' test scores did not seem to be influenced by family size.

In another set of studies (Durkin, 1961; 1966; Plessas & Oakes, 1964), researchers analyzed the contributions of family members to the development of reading skills in children who learned to read before school entrance. In general, children who learned to read early were read to frequently by members of their families and had parents who answered their reading-related questions. Durkin's samples of early readers in California and New York included children from a broad range of socioeconomic backgrounds. Although more mothers of early readers were college graduates, no simple relationship was found between socioeconomic status and early reading ability. The most striking difference between parents of early readers and nonearly readers was that parents of early readers spent more time with them, read to them more, answered more of their questions, and demonstrated by their own reading behavior that reading is a rich source of relaxation and contentment.

The findings of these studies of early readers indicate that the family background variables associated with the development of outstanding skills among young gifted children are those related to direct parental involvement with their children. Parents who spend time with their children, facilitate their interests, answer their questions, and provide a warm, supportive base for intellectual exploration are likely to foster the development of their children's skills, no matter what the family's economic or social status level.

PHYSICAL DEVELOPMENT

The gifted children identified in Terman's study (1925) were found to be, on the whole, physically superior to national standardization samples. They were taller, heavier, stronger, had greater lung capacity, and tended to be healthier than average children the same age. Other researchers (see, e.g., Barbe, 1955) have also noted the physical superiority of gifted children. These findings have been criticized, however, as being artifacts of biased sampling procedures. Hildreth (1954) and others have commented that the supposed physical superiority of gifted children may be due to the fact that most gifted children in these studies have come from upper socioeconomic backgrounds, where nutrition and health care practices tend to be superior to those in the general population. Frierson (1965) found no height or weight differences between gifted and average children drawn from the same regional populations. Klausmeier (1958) found no differences between high achieving and low achieving third and fifth graders in height, weight, strength of grip, number of permanent teeth, and carpal (wrist bone) development. Likewise, Laycock and Caylor (1964) found no differences in height, weight, leg circumference, or shoulder or pelvic girth of gifted fourth- through sixth-grade children when compared with siblings whose IQs were at least 20 points lower. The gifted children in this study were selected for Binet IQs above 120 or California Test of Mental Maturity IQs above 130.

Given these data, it seems inappropriate to include physical superiority on a checklist of characteristics of gifted children when the ultimate criterion for giftedness is superior intellectual ability. It should be noted that in each of the studies mentioned above, the gifted population was chosen for high scores on some measure of intellectual or academic achievement. It may be that a group of children identified as gifted on the basis of advanced psychomotor skills would show generally superior physical development. There is no good evidence, however, that superior physical development is related to superior intellectual development.

It should also be noted that none of the aforementioned studies focused on the development of gifted preschool-aged children. One study (Leithwood, 1971) of preschool-aged children did find some interesting results. Among 60 four-year-old children enrolled in two Toronto nursery schools, a relationship was found between Binet IQ and ability to perform complex motor tasks as measured by a test of gymnastic sequences. This test measured children's ability to perform both concurrent and asynchronous sequences of actions. In contrast, there was no relationship between IQ and performance on simple motor tasks involving measures of strength, flexibility, balance, gross body coordination, and energy mobilization. The children's intellectual skills were generally advanced: the mean IQ of the group was 125. It may well be, then, that children's performance on motor tasks is related to general cognitive ability to the extent that the tasks involve cognitive organization. Measures of general physical growth, however, do not at any age show a relationship to measures of general cognitive growth.

EARLY DEVELOPMENT

Precocious development during infancy has also been reported to be characteristic of intellectually gifted children. The children in Terman's (1925) sample, for example, walked and talked at earlier ages than average according to their parents' retrospective reports. These findings, however, have not been replicated. In the longitudinal study of intellectually advanced children in Seattle, no relationship has been found between parents' retrospective reports of early developmental milestones such as walking, talking, and intellectual precocity during the preschool years (Krinsky, Jackson, & Robinson, 1977). One possibility is that the parents' memories of when such milestones occurred are simply not accurate enough to permit demonstration of existing relationships. Results from the longitudinal Collaborative Perinatal Project in Boston indicate, however, that the lack of predication of superior intelligence from developmental milestones achieved in infancy may be due to lack of continuity among these aspects of development rather than to faulty parental memory. This study (Willerman & Fiedler, 1977) included 114 children who scored at 140 or above on the Binet at age four. These children were only slightly advanced on the Bayley Scales of Infant Development given at eight months, and their Bayley scores were not correlated with their Binet IQs. Their high scores at age four could not have been predicted by the indices of development collected during infancy.

SOCIAL AND EMOTIONAL DEVELOPMENT

Assessment of Social and Emotional Development

The emotional characteristics and social interaction abilities of young children show striking individual differences that are important determinants of their adjustment in many situations. Questions concerning social maturity become crucial when decisions are to be made about school placement. In determining whether an intellectually advanced four-year-old, for example, is a good candidate for early entrance to kindergarten, it is not sufficient to know that the child's academic skills are at an advanced level. One must also make some prediction about how the child will function as a social and emotional being in the context of the kindergarten classroom.

It is difficult, however, to make reliable and valid assessments of the social and emotional adjustment of young children. Many of the existing measures of social maturity ask questions more related to cognitive abilities than to actual social behaviors. For example, the social scale of the Alpern and Boll Development Profile (Alpren & Boll, 1972), an interview assessment procedure in which a parent describes a child's behaviors in a variety of domains, includes such items as whether or not the child can define his or her own gender and whether or not the child can draw a recognizable person.

Measures that rely on parents to describe their children's behaviors may be biased by the parents' limited perspectives or faulty memories. Measures in which children themselves are asked to respond to a questionnaire or to answer questions in an interview are usually inappropriate for use with young children. Even when children are intellectually advanced, they often lack the verbal facility to respond adequately in such situations. They frequently select the final alternative of multiple choice items and sometimes tend to choose either "yes" or "no" as a consistent response regardless of question content (Gorsuch, Henighan, & Barnard, 1972; Roedell, Slaby, & Robinson, 1977). Many measures are severely limited because they have low reliability and questionable validity (Walker, 1973). In fact, in investigating instruments for use in evaluating Head Start programs, researchers from the Huron Institute (Walker, Bane, & Bryk, 1973) have concluded that none of the available measures of social and emotional growth in young children is adequate.

Measurement of young children's social development, then, is far from a desirable level of precision. The basic problem lies in the nature of the task. When measuring intellectual development in young children, one attempts to discover optimum situations that will allow children to show their best performance. The goal is to discover what each child is capable of doing, given ideal conditions. The goal in social skills assessment, on the other hand, is usually to determine a child's typical performance in a variety of situations, rather than to determine absolute levels of competence. The probability of a specifiable behavior occurring in a particular setting depends to a large extent on the circumstances in that setting. The intellectually advanced child, for example, who is bored by the activities of the regular classroom may be inattentive, listless, or possibly disruptive. Placed in a more challenging situation, the same child may be deeply involved, eager, and attentive. Ratings of such a child in the first situation would be expected to differ radically from ratings based on the second situation (Roedell, 1977b).

Instead of assessing a child's general level of social maturity, it may be more meaningful to define which behaviors are required for success in particular settings and to observe a child in those settings. An interview with a strange adult is hardly likely to provide a good index of how a child will behave with classroom peers. Furthermore, children are likely to behave very differently in strange situations than in familiar ones. For example, parents of one five-year-old child, who was asked to "sit in" on a first grade class to see "how well he would fit," reported that the child was judged socially immature when he failed to rush out to the playground with the other children at recess time—a classroom routine totally unfamiliar to him (Roedell, 1977b).

These limitations in definition and measurement of social and emotional development should be borne in mind when evaluating the literature reviewed here. In spite of difficulties, however, a substantial body of research data does exist and can provide some insights into the everyday behavior of gifted children.

Personality Characteristics of Gifted Children

There have been numerous descriptions of the social and personality characteristics of young, intellectually gifted children. Hildreth's (1938) conclusion that "the gifted child can be identified on the basis of certain behavior signs and trends, as well as through outcomes from standardized tests," has become dogma among many educators. Hildreth's observations were derived from comments made by testers during the administration of the Stanford-Binet to three- and four-year-old children enrolled in a private school in New York. Children who scored above 130 were compared with children who scored between 90 and 110 in terms of their described performance during the testing situation. It is not surprising that many more positive characteristics were noted for high IQ children than for children with more modest scores. To achieve high IQ scores, children must first respond to the test session as a fruitful and productive experience. The fact that children with high test scores were noted to be superior to average children in personality characteristics, such as cooperation, persistence in the face of difficult problems, enthusiasm, patience, maturity, responsiveness, and resistance to fatigue, probably tells us little about the behavior of either group of children in nontest situations.

Data from a broad range of studies indicate that within any group of gifted children, there can be found profound individual differences in personal and social characteristics (Gallagher, 1975). Small mean differences were found by Terman between his group and comparison groups on several measures of social and personality development. Nevertheless, Terman and his co-workers consistently stressed the wide variety of personality characteristics among gifted children (see, e.g., Terman & Oden, 1947). Studies in which the personalities of bright children were measured with the Rorschach test have also demonstrated considerable variability (Mensh, 1950). At the Seattle project's Child Development Preschool, teachers' impressions of the social abilities of 30 intellectually advanced children were collected via the California Preschool Social Competency rating scale (Levine, Elzey, & Lewis, 1969). Teacher ratings, which yielded percentile ranks ranging from the twenty-first percentile to the ninety-eighth percentile, showed a diverse range of social competencies.

Other studies have found that some of the personality characteristics attributed to bright children may in fact be related to their high socioeconomic status. Bonsall (1955) found that most differences in temperament in a sample of twelfth grade boys were related to socioeconomic status rather than to IQ. Davidson (1943) found that characteristics such as responsiveness to outside stimuli, certain fears, wishes, and worries were related to socioeconomic status. In her sample of 102 highly intelligent children, she found "as wide a variation in ... personality characteristics as probably would be found in any group of children" (p. 170).

Definitions of giftedness necessarily play a large part in determining which social and personality characteristics may be relevant to a description of gifted children. If gifted children are identified in terms of superior leadership qualities, then certain social characteristics will more likely be evident. Renzulli and Hartman (1971) found, for example, that students identified by a teacher questionnaire for leadership qualities also received high scores on sociometric ratings given by their peers. Children identified as creative might be judged by different characteristics than children identified as high academic achievers. In a study of kindergarten children, for example, Singer and Rummo (1973) studied the relationships between creativity, IQ, and behavioral style. They found that highly creative children were rated low on work orientation characteristics such as autonomy, task persistence, and acceptance of responsibility. Highly creative boys were rated higher on communicativeness, curiosity and novelty-seeking, humorous, playful attitudes, and emotional expressiveness. Girls who were high in both creativity and IQ and girls who were low in both creativity and IQ showed less self-confidence and involvement in classroom activities and were less accepted by their peers than girls high in only one of these dimensions.

Overall Adjustment of Gifted Children

Several studies agree that, whatever their particular personality characteristics, children with moderately advanced intellectual skills tend to be well-adjusted. They are socially adept, emotionally secure, and do well both in school and in later life (Gallagher, 1958a; 1975; Hollingworth, 1942; Liddle, 1958; Terman, 1925). There is general agreement, however, that children with extremely advanced intellectual skills may have more difficulty in finding a comfortable niche in society (Getzels & Dillon, 1973; Hollingworth, 1942; Newland, 1976; Terman & Oden, 1974).

Several factors might explain the greater problems experienced by children with extremely advanced intellectual abilities. In the first place, there may be a wide gap between the levels of their intellectual and their physical development. In the Seattle project, for example, we have seen preschool children who read at the fourth-grade level but who have difficulty manipulating a pencil. While some of the Seattle children are physically as well as intellectually advanced, others display the physical awkwardness and lack of coordination typical of their agemates (Roedell & Robinson, 1977). Intellectually advanced children may conceptualize projects that are too complex for them to complete with their limited physical skills. The results can be extreme frustration at the lack of perfection in the finished product.

The intellectual-social gap created when children's intellectual capacities outstrip their level of social maturity can also create problems for young children. People may become irritated with children when their social skills fall short of the expectations generated by their intellectual maturity. Some intellectually advanced children, it is true, may demonstrate comparably advanced social sensitivity. However, many three- and four-year-olds with mental ages of seven and eight still need help toileting and dressing, tend to hit and kick other children when frustrated, have trouble communicating needs and feelings to other children, lack the skill to initiate cooperative play or to join a group, have not learned to share and take turns, and so on (Roedell & Robinson, 1977). In short, these children are socially similar to three- and four-year-olds of average intelligence. At the same time, they think and reason like much older children.

This unevenness in developmental levels may be particularly difficult for young children who often must cope either with being more advanced in intellectual ability than many of their agemates, or with being the youngest in a group of older children who are their intellectual peers. Such children are necessarily isolated by their unusual abilities and must learn to make adjustments for the lesser skills of their same-age peers (Hollingworth, 1942; O'Shea, 1960). The mother of one four-year-old boy in the Child Development Preschool reported that her son wrote a note to hang on the front door, telling his friends that he did not want to play. He then crumpled the note and sadly confided to his mother, "I can't hang this note up, Mom. They can't read!" Another parent reported that her four-year-old son was frustrated when his neighborhood friends failed to keep appointments he had made with them; it was difficult for him to accept that they had not yet learned to tell time.

Patterns of Temperament

The ways in which gifted children adjust to their environment may be influenced by individual differences in temperament. Thomas and Chess (1977) describe temperament as "the *how* of behavior. It differs from ability ... and from motivation ... (and) concerns the *way* in which an individual behaves"

(p. 9). Buss and Plomin (1975) explain that temperament, or behavioral style, refers to whether a response is "fast or slow, mild or intense, sparse and un-elaborated, or adorned and elaborated, etc. Temperament generally deals more with the stylistic aspects of behavior . . ." than with behavioral content (p. 5).

In 1956 Thomas and Chess (1963; 1977) began a longitudinal study of middle and working class children living in New York City. On the basis of data collected from parents, coupled with observations of these children and interviews with their teachers, Thomas and Chess identified three temperament constellations that may have clinical significance with respect to gifted children's adjustment patterns. The *easy child* is characterized by regularity, positive approach responses to new events, mild, generally positive moods, and high adaptability to change. Such children easily develop regular schedules, are pleasant to be around, and are usually the delight of parents and teachers. The *difficult child* represents the opposite end of each continuum. Such children show irregularity in biological functions, are intense, frequently display negative moods, have difficulty adapting to change, and show intensely negative responses to new situations. These are the children who laugh loudly when happy and scream violently when upset. The third pattern characterizes the *slow-to-warm-up child*. Such children show mildly negative responses to new stimuli and adapt slowly if given a chance to experience new events repeatedly. Of course, not all children fall neatly into one of these three temperament groups.

Thomas and Chess (1963; 1977) indicate that they have found no relationship in their longitudinal sample between children's IQs and their temperament characteristics. Nevertheless, many checklists used to identify gifted children include characteristics that are actually temperament traits. Gifted children are often described, for example, as being persistent, having a long attention span, being responsive to new stimuli, and so on (e.g., Abraham, 1976; Hildreth, 1938).

Using a temperament questionnaire developed by Thomas and Chess on the basis of their longitudinal sample, Macey (1978) found that parents of gifted children in the Seattle project described them as varying widely on temperament characteristics. These findings are consistent with a broad range of data that indicate it is not possible to be accurate in describing gifted children as a group on nonintellective variables. A more fruitful area of study may be the investigation of the implications of individual differences among gifted children in personality and temperament. Thomas and Chess (1970) suggest that behavioral adjustment is the result of the interaction between children's temperament and their environment. The temperament characteristics of bright children may play a deciding role in determining their successful adjustment to different environments. Several children may perform academic tasks, for example, with equal competence, but may differ radically from one another in their stylistic approach. One child may attack a problem with great intensity and persistence, while another may approach the same problem quietly and with a certain amount of diffidence. Still another may be easily distracted by outside stimuli and may work in repeated spurts of activity with frequent breaks between each effort (Chess, Thomas, & Cameron, 1976). High activity children may have difficulty conforming to the demands of a structured classroom. Children who tend to warm up slowly may not master the content of new learning situations as quickly as their IQs indicate they might. Such children need time to overcome their initial withdrawal reactions. Once they have adapted to the new material, their understanding may be even greater than that of children who seemed to grasp the problem more quickly (Chess, 1968; Chess, Thomas, & Cameron, 1976).

Teachers tend to interpret a child's hesitancy to encounter new material as either inadequate intellectual capacity or underlying anxiety (Chess, 1968). They tend to underestimate the intelligence of children who show initial negative reactions to new situations (Thomas & Chess, 1977). In one study, Gordon and Thomas (1967) asked kindergarten teachers to rate the intelligence of the children in their class, and to classify them according to temperament characteristics. Four categories of temperament were established: 1) *plungers* were children who plunged into new things quickly and positively; 2) *go-alongers* were children who went along with the group in a generally positive manner; 3) *sideliners* were children who waited and then gradually became involved in new activities; and 4) *nonparticipators* were children who remained negative to new situations for weeks, months, or indefinitely. Intelligence tests given the children revealed that teachers were biased in their judgments of intelligence by their perceptions of the children's temperament. Most of the plungers had average IQs, but they tended to be rated as above average by teachers. Of 30 children who had superior IQs, only seven were plungers, and six of these were correctly rated as above average in intelligence. All four of the bright children who were sideliners were *incorrectly* estimated as being average in intelligence. In general, plungers were more likely to be judged intelligent than were sideliners.

The underestimation of ability by teachers can have damaging effects on bright children. In a study (Pringle, 1970) of 103 bright children brought to a clinic because of general maladjustment, it was found that most of them had teachers who underestimated their ability and did not encourage them. The most frequent symptom presented by these "able misfits" was a lack of confidence. Case studies have also chronicled the difficulties of bright children who are not perceived as bright by their teachers. Ogilvie (1973), for example, described a child with an IQ of 170 who had a highly distractible temperament and was very active. His teachers could not be convinced that he was particularly bright.

Teachers need to learn that advanced intellectual skills are not always accompanied by positive temperament styles. Parents of bright but slow-to-warm-up or negative children might do well to be sure that their children's teachers are informed about their advanced intellectual talents, since the teachers may well underestimate their children's abilities to handle challenging assignments. The resulting mismatch between the child's ability and the academic curriculum provided may result in boredom and an increase in the original negative behavior.

Development of Social Cognition

One of the areas in which a relationship between social skills and intellectual skills might be expected is the area of social cognition—children's understanding of their social world. Children's ability to understand what another person thinks, feels, sees, and intends and their ability to describe other people are developmental phenomena. These aspects of social cognition change in predictable ways as children grow older. To a large extent, the way children behave in social settings may be related to their understanding of those settings (Shantz, 1975). It seems logical that children with generally precocious intellectual skills might develop a mature understanding of other people's thoughts, emotions, intentions, and viewpoints at a correspondingly early age.

Moderate relationships have usually been found between children's intelligence as measured by intelligence tests and their ability to understand another person's point of view or their ability to describe other people (Coie & Dorval, 1973; Irwin & Ambron, 1973; Lively & Bromley, 1973; Rothenberg, 1970; Rubin, 1973; Shantz, 1975). These relationships may vary, however, with the gender of the children, their socioeconomic class, and the type of intelligence test used (Shantz, 1975).

Development of the concept of gender is one aspect of social cognition that has been shown to be related to the general intellectual development of young children. Children's understanding of gender has been shown to develop in a four-stage sequence, as measured by a gender constancy test. This test consists of a series of questions that determine a child's ability to classify correctly the sex of self and of others (gender identity) and to demonstrate an understanding of the invariance of a person's sex over time (gender stability) and across situations (gender consistency). Young children who have not yet developed a complete concept of gender may be able to tell whether they are a boy or a girl but may indicate that they will change sex if they wear clothes or play with toys appropriate to the opposite sex. They may also state that they can grow up to become a different sexed adult if they want to. Children's level of gender constancy has been shown to predict the amount of time they will spend watching characters of the same sex in a movie and is believed to be related to a child's general sex-role development (Slaby & Frey, 1975).

In a recent study, Miller, Roedell, Slaby, and Robinson (1978) investigated the concept of gender in a group of three- and four-year-old children, some of whom were intellectually gifted. They found a strong positive relationship between development of the gender concept and general cognitive development. In addition, children whose IQs were at or above 130 answered significantly more gender constancy items correctly and, in fact, were one full stage higher in their understanding of gender than children the same age whose IQs were below 130.

Development of Social Interaction Skills

Roedell (1978) investigated the social interaction skills of a group of intellectually advanced three- through five-year-old children whose average IQ was 138. Three measures of social skills were taken: the Preschool Interpersonal Problem-solving Test (PIPS), teacher ratings of each child's behavior using the Hahnemann Preschool Behavior Rating Scale, and observations of ongoing social behavior during free activity time in the Child Development Preschool. Previous research (Spivack & Shure, 1974) has demonstrated a relationship between the ability to conceptualize alternative solutions to social conflict situations, as measured on the PIPS test, and the general classroom adjustment of disadvantaged preschool children. In contrast to these data, Roedell found no relationship between performance on the PIPS test and either teachers' ratings of children's adjustment or observations of children's free play behavior. While all three measures elicited a wide range of performance within the gifted group, IQ was related only to those measures that involved cognitive aspects of socialization. For example, children with the highest IQs had more ideas about ways children might solve theoretical social conflicts and had more ideas about ways for children to interact cooperatively. However, these advanced social cognitive skills were not reflected in the children's behavior. It is possible that a more sensitive observation code might reveal differences in social behavior related to differences in cognitive ability.

It seems, however, that problem-solving ability alone is not sufficient to guarantee appropriate social interaction behavior. The strongest influence on behavior in this study was the time of year the assessments were made. Children were generally more social and engaged in more cooperative interaction at the end of the year, after participating in a program that emphasized the teaching of social interaction skills through teacher guidance and general positive reinforcement procedures. Social experience, then, must be added to social understanding to ensure the development of good social interaction skills.

Friendship and Popularity

There is some conflict in the literature concerning the popularity, or lack of it, of gifted children. Some argue that gifted children tend to be isolated from their peers (O'Shea, 1960); others declare that gifted children are likely to have friends and to be well-liked (Gallagher, 1958a; 1958b).

Levels of peer acceptance usually have been measured by sociometric instruments. In a typical sociometric assessment, researchers ask all children in a group to nominate the child they would most like to interact with, i.e., the one they would most like to have near them at a school party, to help with homework, or to be on the same team (Mann, 1957). Frequently children are also asked to nominate those children they would least like to associate with. A child's popularity score is the total number of positive nominations received from classmates.

In general, research supports the claim that bright children tend to be popular (Gallagher, 1958a; 1958b; 1975; Hartup, 1970; Heber, 1956). In studies that have examined the relationship between IQs and scores on sociometric tests, the correlations are usually positive and significant, although they range from a fairly low .20 to a moderately high .65 (Hartup, 1970).

In addition, it has been found that bright children tend to be better able to predict both their own social status and the status of their peers (Gallagher, 1958b; Miller, 1956). These self-assessment skills may be further evidence of generally advanced social cognition among bright children and may also help to explain their popularity. Children who understand the needs of others are more likely to be sensitive to those needs.

Gallagher (1975) points out that intellectually advanced children "are usually popular or unpopular for the same kinds of reasons that other children are popular or unpopular" (p. 39). Bright children with good social interaction skills are more likely to be popular than bright children who lack such skills.

While popularity and peer acceptance may be the reality for many bright children, alienation and peer rejection are the fate of other bright children, particularly those with extraordinarily advanced abilities (Gallagher, 1975; Getzels & Dillon, 1973; Hollingworth, 1942; Miller, 1956; Newland, 1976; Terman & Oden, 1947). Gallagher (1958a), for example, demonstrated that while moderately bright elementary school children tend to be popular with a broad range of their fellow students, children with IQs above 165 are relatively unpopular with their classmates.

O'Shea (1960) and Hollingworth (1942) suggest that the social isolation of extraordinarily advanced students may be attributed to problems of communication. This difficulty may be even more pronounced among those unusually bright children who are of preschool age. A three-year-old, for example, who can communicate needs and ideas using complex sentences and the vocabulary of a six-year-old may find it hard to relate to same-age peers with more limited linguistic abilities. A four-year-old whose passion is playing games such as checkers and monopoly may not find same-age playmates with similar tastes and skills.

The potential isolation of bright children can be alleviated if they are placed in company with other children who have the same level of abilities. O'Shea (1960) cites several studies that indicate that friendships are more likely to be formed among young children of like mental age than among children who are of similar chronological age. Hubbard (1929) found a positive correlation of .41 between the mental ages of pairs of three-year-olds who played together frequently and an even stronger correlation of .62 between the mental ages of children who were especially good friends.

Among older children, however, the evidence is not consistent. Gallagher (1958a) found that the strongest determinant of friendship in one elementary school was propinquity rather than IQ. Children tended to choose as best friends children who lived in their neighborhoods. Bright children were equally likely to choose bright and average children for friends. Mann (1957), on the other hand, found that elementary school students who spent half their time in a program for gifted children and the remainder of their school day in a regular classroom concentrated their choices of both "best liked" and "least liked" companions among classmates in the gifted program. The gifted students indicated a general lack of interest in their less intellectually able classmates from the regular program. Apparently these children were simply not interesting enough to arouse either strong liking or strong antipathy. The results of this study may have been biased, however, by the fact that the sociometric assessment was done during a session of the gifted program.

In short, it seems that the popularity of young gifted children is related to individual differences in their patterns of social interaction skills, in the extremity and type of advancement in their abilities, and in the availability of similarly able children to provide intellectual peers.

PATTERNS OF INTELLECTUAL ABILITY

Among educators who work with children of superior intellectual ability, there is a strong conviction that gifted children think in ways that are qualitatively different from the ways in which average children think. Newland (1976), for example, states that gifted children are "particularly capable of quick and generally accurate generalization;" that they can learn highly abstract symbols with great speed, and deduce complex relationships among them; and that they have superior memories.

Jackson (1979) has observed that this description illustrates the level of our understanding of the thought processes of intellectually superior children. It is, on the one hand, an excellent description; virtually anyone who has worked with intellectually superior children of any age would accept it as an accurate and useful description of their behavior. However, it fails to include mention of the fact that all of the characteristics specified are characteristics that distinguish older from younger children equally as well as they distinguish brighter from less bright children. The description implies a qualitative difference in the thinking of intellectually superior children, but it actually says only that such children are developmentally advanced.

Intellectually superior children are defined by measures designed to quantify developmental advancement. In fact, the more accurate label for such children is "intellectually advanced." Most standard intelligence tests are based on the developmental rate model first established by Binet in his original measures of intelligence (as noted in Chapter 1). This model describes the development of intelligence as a function of the age of individuals. Children who earn high scores on standard tests of intelligence or academic ability do so by performing tasks typically mastered only by older children. The system of equating intellectual superiority with intellectual precocity breaks down in adolescence. It makes little sense to say that a bright 15-year-old has a mental age of 23. From the middle teens on, individual differences are largely, though not entirely, independent of age differences (Baltes, 1977). Using the developmental rate model, individual differences among adults can be explained by the assumption that intellectually superior adults have continued to develop intellectually beyond the level at which their less able contemporaries stopped progressing.

Developmental psychologists continue to revise their appraisals of which processes characterize the essence of developmental differences. However, Jackson (1979) concludes that most recent research supports the position that with increasing age children become better able to solve problems in systematic ways, to transfer what is learned in one situation to other, similar situations, to increase their capacity to deal with large amounts of new information and to solve complex problems by interrelating such information, and to cope more efficiently with logical problems that are independent of, or contradicted by, perceptual evidence. These developmental differences, which describe the changes that take place as children grow older, seem identical to the differences between gifted and average children proposed by many educators.

As part of the longitudinal study of intellectually advanced children under way in Seattle, many young children have been identified who do seemingly extraordinary things. Some can use very complex language forms before they are two; others have learned to read fluently by the age of three; some can complete 100-piece jigsaw puzzles at the age of three; and so on. None of these behaviors is remarkable in itself. The extraordinary point is that they are performed by children who are so young (Robinson, 1977).

Certainly there must be some differences between the learning processes of intellectually superior children and those of average ability. If there were no such differences, all children growing up in similar environments would develop at approximately the same rate. Recent studies of information processing in children and adults of different ability levels have suggested several mechanisms that might mediate individual differences in performance on psycho-metric tests, but the data are far from sufficient to generate a complete picture of qualitative differences between gifted and average children.

Types of Intellectual Ability

Researchers working with the Seattle longitudinal study have paid partic-ular attention to individual differences in the types of advanced intellectual skills demonstrated by young children and to how parents' and teachers' descriptions of these children relate to test scores. The group of primary interest in this study is comprised of the 53 children who have demonstrated extraordinary intellec-tual precocity before they are six years old. Extraordinary precocity has been defined as performance four or more standard deviations above the mean, or at the norm for children twice the child's age, on any of several measures of gener-al or specific intellectual abilities. These measures are described in Chapter 3. Typical cases meeting the criterion of extraordinary performance include a three-year-old child whose Binet IQ was above 164 and a four-year-old whose reading ability as measured by the PIAT (Peabody Individual Achievement Test) was at the level of the average nine-year-old in the fourth grade of elementary school.

The 53 children have demonstrated their precocity in different areas or combinations of areas. Some of the children have demonstrated consistent pre-cocity in repeated test sessions over a period of several years, while others have performed at extraordinarily advanced levels on one occasion only. The variety of patterns is demonstrated in Table 2-1 (Robinson, Jackson, & Roedell, 1978).

In most cases, individual differences in patterns of test performance are confirmed by children's classroom behavior. For example, according to the re-ports of teachers in the Child Development Preschool, certain children have been particularly proficient in logical, mathematical reasoning, in developing sym-metrical designs with pattern blocks or with painting and drawing materials, in drawing maps, and similar activities. These children are usually the same chil-dren who have scored high on standard tests of spatial reasoning ability. During one mathematics lesson, children were asked to work in pairs making designs from pattern blocks. One child was to create the design, while the other child copied the design with his or her own set of blocks. Most children could carry out this task using patterns of four or five blocks. One pair of children, however, could successfully exchange designs made with eight or nine blocks. Both of these children have also demonstrated extraordinary spatial ability on standard-ized tests.

In contrast, another child with a Binet IQ that extends beyond the limits of the scale to an estimated 177 showed less extraordinary spatial reasoning scores; her highest performances on the Binet were on verbal reasoning items. This child was not remarkably proficient in map-making or design-copying. She

Table 2-1
Patterns of Extraordinary Precocity
Demonstrated by Children Aged Six and Under
1974–1978

Areas of Extraordinary Precocity	Girls	Boys	Total
IQ Only (total instance = 18)	6	1	7
Spatial Reasoning Only (Total instances = 11)	1	4	5
Memory Only (Total instances = 22)	7	10	17
Reading Only (Total instances = 18)	3	3	6
IQ and Spatial Reasoning	0	3	3
IQ and Memory	0	1	1
IQ and Reading	2	2	4
IQ, Reading, and Mathematics	1	0	1
IQ, Spatial Reasoning, and Reading	0	1	1
Reading and Memory	0	3	3
Reading and Mathematics	0	1	1
Mathematics and Memory	1	0	1
IQ and Mathematics	0	1	1
Spatial Reasoning and Reading	0	2	2
Totals	21	32	53

NOTE: The "total instances" in parentheses under each single ability classification refer to the frequency of extraordinary performance in this classification if children extraordinary in more than one area are counted for each ability.

did, however, read at the fourth grade level at the age of four. Her favorite books at that time were *The Little House* series by Laura Ingalls Wilder—a series with many words and few pictures, designed for elementary school-aged children. This girl also has enjoyed making up elaborate fantasy dramas involving several characters and complicated plots. The comparative strengths in verbal skills indicated in her test scores are also evident in her everyday behavior (Roedell, 1977a).

Development of Academic Skills

The impressive thing about the academic abilities of gifted preschoolers is the extreme diversity of skill patterns. The early acquisition of advanced academic skills does not seem to be totally determined by IQ or mental age. In the longitudinal study in Seattle, for example, preschool-aged children have been identified who scored above 160 on IQ tests but who had not yet learned to read or to compute, while other children with IQ scores as low as 116 were fluent readers by the age of three. The range of IQs of early readers studied by Durkin (1966) was also wide—the group in New York ranged from 82 to 170, and the group in California from 91 to 161. These and other data on children who read early are discussed in detail in Chapter 3.

An even more striking example of diversity in academic skills is the performance on the Peabody Individual Achievement Test (Dunn & Markwardt, 1970) of 23 intellectually advanced children enrolled in the Child Development Preschool in Seattle compared with an unselected group of preschool children. The mean IQ of the precocious group was 145. The unselected sample attended a nearby preschool in the same neighborhood. Not surprisingly, the children in the Child Development Preschool performed significantly better than children in the comparison group. On the average, the precocious three-year-olds performed at the level of beginning kindergarteners, and the four-year-olds at the first grade level.

However, the range of levels of academic competence was far greater in the precocious preschool sample than in the unselected group of preschoolers. In the unselected group, performance ranged from the preschool level to the first grade level. In the precocious sample, performance ranged from the preschool level to the third grade level. On individual subtests, the disparity in range was even greater. In reading recognition, for example, the top score for any child in the unselected group was at the first grade level, while the top score in the precocious group was at the fourth grade level (Roedell, 1977a; Shorr, Jackson, & Robinson, 1978).

Do children with early acquisition of academic skills show different patterns of performance in later years? There is little evidence concerning this question. Durkin (1966), however, found that after six years of school instruction in reading, children who had read before entering first grade still maintained their lead in achievement over classmates of the same mental age who did not begin to read until the first grade. This does not, of course, imply that parents or teachers should push young children into learning to read. The children who read early in the Durkin study learned mainly on their own initiative, with some help from parents given in answers to their questions. There is no evidence that pushing children who are not yet interested in learning to read is a beneficial exercise. Such an endeavor would most likely lead to negative attitudes about reading and learning in general and might well result in lowered achievement later on.

SUMMARY

Much of the literature concerning gifted children provides checklists of family, personal, social, and intellectual characteristics supposedly associated with giftedness. In reality, however, there are vast individual differences among gifted children in all these areas. Gifted children can be found in all ethnic and socioeconomic groups. When socioeconomic status is controlled for, children gifted in intellectual areas are not markedly different from average children in their physical development. While some intellectually precocious children learn to walk and talk at earlier ages than average, others do not.

Gifted children show a wide range of personality characteristics and levels of social maturity. While children with moderately advanced intellectual abilities often show good overall adjustment, children with extremely advanced intellectual skills may have more difficulty. Adjustment problems may, in some cases, result from the uneven development that occurs when intellectual capabilities far outstrip the child's levels of physical or social development. Children with advanced intellectual skills sometimes tend to show advanced understanding of social situations and to be better able to judge other people's feelings. Intellectually advanced preschoolers, however, may need guided social experience to help them make use of their advanced social understanding.

Individual differences in general patterns of temperament may be important factors in the later adjustment of bright children. Teachers tend to underestimate the intelligence of children who are slow to approach new activities. A bright child who is very hesitant in interpersonal situations may not receive needed encouragement to attempt challenging tasks.

Some descriptions of gifted children suggest that they think in qualitatively different ways from average children. However, most of the characteristics used to describe the difference between gifted and average children's thought processes are similar to characteristics used to describe differences between older and younger children.

Some intellectually advanced children acquire proficiency in basic academic skills at an early age; others do not. Some children with advanced intellectual ability show superior skill in most or even all cognitive domains; others show advanced skills only in particular areas, such as verbal reasoning, memory, or spatial reasoning ability. In patterns of intellectual precocity, as in all other areas, the most striking characteristic of gifted children is their diversity.

3

IDENTIFICATION OF GIFTED PERFORMANCE IN YOUNG CHILDREN

THERE CAN BE no single system of identification that is appropriate for all preschool programs for gifted children. An identification system makes sense only if the selection criteria are matched to the objectives and content of the program the children will attend. If the program emphasizes the development of intellectual abilities and academic skills, then selection must be based on children's performance on measures of these abilities. If a program is designed to serve children with particular talents, such as musical ability, then assessment of children's ability in that realm would be the most reasonable identification procedure.

Identification procedures may involve activities such as the administration of standard tests, the evaluation of information from parents and teachers, direct observation of the child's behavior, or review of the child's creative work. Each of these approaches has both strengths and weaknesses. The most effective identification systems combine several types of procedures that complement one another.

IDENTIFICATION BY STANDARD TEST PERFORMANCE

For many years, standard tests have played a major role in systems for identifying children for special education programs. Indeed, the first intelligence tests were designed to pick out children who would not be likely to succeed in the regular educational system. These tests are still widely used. There are, though, increasingly strong arguments against reliance on a test score as the *only* criterion by which a child is selected for a special program. The identification procedures adopted for many programs for gifted children supplement standard test measures of intellectual ability, academic achievement, or creativity with other types of information.

Standard tests are popular identification instruments because they offer

---

The principal author of this chapter is Nancy Ewald Jackson.

an opportunity to compare an individual child's performance with the performance of other children the same age who have been given exactly the same questions to answer or problems to solve. An identification process usually involves selecting a few children from a larger pool of applicants to a popular program. Any measure that maximizes the opportunity to make objective and fair comparisons of the abilities of the applicants is, therefore, bound to be highly desirable. Unfortunately, no standard test provides a completely fair and appropriate index of comparison for all children. There are, however, a few principles that can be applied to judge how closely a particular test is likely to conform to that ideal.

An Introduction to Standard Tests

In evaluating a standard test, the first question is the test's validity. Validity simply means that a test measures what it purports to measure. Validity takes several forms, depending upon what the test is measuring.

To be valid, a standard academic achievement test must measure the real-life behavior it purports to measure. A standard test of reading skill, for example, would have little validity if it was unrelated to the children's everyday reading performance in the classroom and at home. Sometimes the extent to which a test measures real-life behavior is evaluated by looking at the actual content of the test. If a test of reading or mathematics skill contains questions about topics that are representative of the classroom curriculum, then it is likely to have some validity simply by virtue of its appropriate content. This is called *face* validity.

Some tests may be valid even though the content of the tests is apparently arbitrary and unrelated to real-life goals. This tends to be typical of intelligence tests, as opposed to academic achievement tests. The validity of intelligence tests for children rests primarily on their ability to predict school performance. Whether a child can quickly and accurately trace a pencil maze (a subtest of the Wechsler Preschool and Primary Scale of Intelligence, or WPPSI; Wechsler, 1967) or repeat a string of numbers in an order that is the reverse of the presentation order (a subtest on many intelligence tests) is not, in itself, important. It is hard to imagine an educational program that would have mastery of either of these skills as a goal. Nonetheless, these items, and others like them, can be useful components of tests that do differentiate among children and yield good estimates of how a child is likely to respond to the educational process.

While the ultimate judgment of a test's validity must rest on its success in measuring or predicting behavior that is important in the real world, estimates of validity are sometimes made in terms of how closely performance on the test corresponds to performance on other, usually better established, tests that are supposed to measure the same thing. Thus, designers of a new, easy-to-administer test of general intellectual ability in young children might argue that the test has validity to the extent that the scores obtained discriminate among children in the same way as do scores on widely accepted tests such as the Stanford-Binet (Terman & Merrill, 1973) or the WPPSI.

The validity described so far refers solely to how well a test estimates a child's abilities at the time of testing. This *concurrent* validity can be thought of as the minimum requirement a test should meet. But a warning is in order. In most practical situations, a test is expected both to estimate what a child can do at the time and to predict a child's capabilities months or years later. Generally the shorter the prediction period, the better the prediction. Intelligence tests administered during the early preschool years are not usually good estimates of a child's later intelligence test performance or school achievement. The usefulness of tests as long-term predictors increases dramatically, however, between the ages of three and six years (Bayley, 1949; Sontag, Baker & Nelson, 1958).

It is quite possible that many children identified as intellectually gifted on the basis of test performance at age four would no longer fall within the limits of that definition if retested several years later. This was the case in a long-term study of 95 children who had earned Stanford-Binet IQs above 140 when tested at four years of age (Willerman & Fiedler, 1977). By the age of seven, the group as a whole was still above average in intellectual ability as measured by the 1949 edition of the Wechsler Intelligence Scale for Children, or WISC, and a test of academic achievement, but their superiority was not nearly so marked as it had been at age four. Some of the apparent drop in IQ was probably the result of differences between the Stanford-Binet and the WISC, but it is doubtful that this difference alone accounted for all the discrepancy. The mean WISC IQ of the seven-year-olds was 123, and the group included eight children whose WISC IQs were below 110.

While this study documents only that scores can *drop* over time, it is worth keeping in mind that many children whose four-year-old Binet IQs are below 140 will substantially outstrip the seven-year-old performance of a group selected for Binet IQs above 140 at age four. While the focus here is on providing appropriate programs for gifted preschool-aged children, other bright children should not be denied equally appropriate opportunities later in their lives because their test performances at preschool age were undistinguished.

Data from the Seattle project's longitudinal study have provided dramatic confirmation of the premise that modest test scores have little relation to how extremely well a preschool-aged child might perform on later tests. We found that the individual Stanford-Binet IQs of children tested for the first time at the age of two or three and retested at age four or five, did not show much stability over time. Although the group as a whole maintained and, in fact, tended to increase in performance level, children's first scores accounted for considerably less than half of the variance in their later scores (Jackson, 1978a). Clearly long-term predictive validity is a serious problem in the use of even the best intellectual assessment instruments with bright young children.

To be a useful identification instrument, a test must be reliable as well as valid. There are several ways of defining reliability, but the most important for our purposes is the concept of test-retest reliability. A measure that has high test-retest reliability is one that yields highly similar scores on repeated administrations close together in time. A child who earned a very high score on a particular test the first time it was administered should, if the test is a reliable one, earn a correspondingly high score if the same test were given again a few days or even a few weeks later.

An unreliable test cannot demonstrate concurrent or predictive validity. If children's scores fluctuate wildly because of differences in their mood at the time of testing, the way the test is administered, or any other extraneous factor, the test has little chance of offering a good estimate of the child's real-life abilities either at the time or in the future.

The American Psychological Association (Standards for Educational and Psychological Tests, 1966; 1974) has set stringent standards to be used by anyone marketing a standardized test for use in practical situations where individuals' lives are going to be affected by the test results. A test that meets these standards must satisfy the basic requirements of reliability and validity. In devising tests to evaluate children's skills in areas where there are no standard tests, test-makers, using research literature as a substitute, may offer reasonable solutions to practical problems. However, even if the research results have been encouraging, the practitioner runs a substantial risk by using unstandardized measures. The principal danger is that children's scores will be taken much more seriously than the qualities of the measure warrant. Any identification procedure involves unavoidable elements of chance and error, but the risks of making inappropriate decisions are greatly magnified when the measures used have not been properly validated.

Even when the best tests are administered under the best possible circumstances, chance factors introduce a certain margin of error into test scores. Scores should, therefore, always be interpreted as indicating a range of performance rather than a fixed value. A child who earns a Stanford-Binet IQ of 132 one year and 129 the next has not suffered a developmental setback. Similarly there is little reason to suspect that a child scoring 132 is actually any more capable than another child scoring 129. Practical decisions sometimes have to be made on the basis of absolute cutoff scores and trivial individual differences, but it is helpful to keep in mind that these decisions are arbitrary and, at best, a necessary evil.

Intelligence test scores tend to be less reliable for younger than for older children and less reliable for brighter than for less bright children (McNemar, 1942; Sattler, 1974). There are some technical reasons that influence these patterns, but part of the problem can be understood if one simply contemplates the challenge of getting a lively two-year-old to sit still, pay attention, speak clearly, and cooperate long enough to complete a standard test session. If everything goes perfectly, the child may demonstrate maximum performance and earn a high score. On the other hand, if the child is shy with the examiner, a nap is overdue, or there are any distractions present, the same child's performance could be substantially less remarkable.

As mentioned earlier, one advantage of standard tests is that they can provide a fair comparison among children by presenting each one with an identical set of challenges—that is, if the children all come from a reasonably similar background. When children come from widely different backgrounds, the fairness of tests is open to question. The most obvious case of cultural bias in testing occurs when a child from a bilingual or non-English-speaking background is given a test standardized on a population of native speakers of English. Even if the test does not include items requiring a verbal response, bilingual children may have more difficulty following directions. This is particularly likely to be the case for very young children. At the age of two or three, simply getting the idea of a task can be a major challenge for any child.

Tests such as the Stanford-Binet or WPPSI, which include measures of children's ability to deal with language in subtle and sophisticated ways, may underestimate the abilities of children from bilingual backgrounds even if the children speak English fluently enough to communicate well in everyday situations. On the other hand, a test standardized for speakers of a bilingual child's first language may also be unfair. Several studies have demonstrated, for example, that a Puerto Rican Spanish version of the WISC is inappropriate for bilingual Mexican-American children. The children's scores on the Spanish version are frequently no higher than their scores on the English version, perhaps because of dialect differences between Puerto Rican and Mexican-American Spanish (Sattler, 1974).

Cultural bias can also be a factor distorting the results of standard tests administered to children who are native speakers of English but who are members of a minority group not represented in the standardization population for the test. If a test has not been standardized with a particular cultural group, it cannot be assumed that the test will differentiate among children in that group in the same way as it does among those in the standardization population.

Children from cultural groups not included in the standardization population of a test may not share the experiences and expectancies typical of children within that population. For example, psychologists who administer the Peabody Picture Vocabulary Test, or PPVT, (Dunn, 1970) to Seattle-area children frequently find that a child who has been struggling with less advanced items responds quickly and confidently when asked to point to the picture that illustrates the word "cascade." The correct choice is a picture of a waterfall, but the Seattle children most often point to the picture of a mountain. The designers of the PPVT, which was standardized among children who lived in Nashville, Tennessee, did not anticipate that some children might identify "cascade" with the Cascade Mountain Range of the Pacific Northwest. One item does not, of course, invalidate an entire test, and it is possible that a test can be extremely useful for testing children not represented in the standardization population. Nonetheless, that usefulness is always an empirical question that must be answered by demonstrating the validity of the test for the group being evaluated. (See Hall & Chansky, 1971, and Sattler, 1974, for examples of such validation procedures.)

Recent standardizations of the most well-known intelligence and achievement tests have generally been based on samples of children who were representative of the United States population in terms of geographic region, urban versus rural environment, socioeconomic status, and minority group membership. The manuals for the most recent versions of the Stanford-Binet (Terman & Merrill, 1973), WPPSI (Wechsler, 1967) and Peabody Individual Achievement Test (Dunn & Markwardt, 1970) describe the procedures used in selecting these representative samples. Some of the tests commonly used to yield quick estimates of intellectual ability, such as the Slosson Intelligence Test (Slosson, 1963), and the Raven Progressive Matrices (Raven, 1976), do not have such representative standardizations.

Even when a test has been standardized on an appropriately representative sample, the test may contain items that are likely to be less familiar and therefore more difficult for children from low-income or minority group families. Test items frequently reflect middle-class values and experiences. A child may, for example, be expected to believe that one should forgive an unintentional injury rather than striking back. The vocabulary sections of intelligence tests may contain words such as "lecture," which are probably more familiar to children whose parents are highly educated.

The cultural bias problem is a difficult one, and some would resolve it by abandoning standardized tests as tools for identification or evaluation (Ginsburg, 1972; Kamin, 1974). Another common approach has been to recommend that some tests are less likely than others to be biased against children from low-income or minority group backgrounds. In general, the tests recommended as relatively culture fair are those that do not heavily involve specific cultural knowledge such as vocabulary. They may be nonverbal and abstract in their content (Bruch, 1971; Cox, 1974). While the performance of bilingual children may be generally better on nonverbal than on verbal tests, an identification system that relied only on nonverbal tests might well discriminate against some minority group and bilingual children even more severely than an identification system that included tests with substantial verbal and cultural content. Different tests emphasize different types of intellectual ability, and a minority child whose strengths are primarily in the areas of verbal knowledge and verbal reasoning ability may perform much better on a test that emphasizes those skills than on a test that involves nonverbal reasoning or perceptual skills.

Individual children sometimes earn very high scores on tests that have been labelled as biased against their minority groups. In 1943, for example, a survey of several research samples identified 16 black children who had earned Stanford-Binet IQs above 160 (Jenkins, 1943). More recently, unexpectedly large percentages of low-income Asian children were found to meet the standard test qualifications for New York's junior high school accelerated program for gifted children (Chen & Goon, 1976). Torrey (1969) reports the case of a six-year-old black child from a low-income family who scored at the upper fourth-grade level in reading and the beginning fifth-grade level in spelling on an academic achievement test.

There is nothing remarkable in the fact that minority group children sometimes perform extremely well on standard tests of intellectual ability and academic achievement. These findings have been cited here simply to demonstrate that these standard tests can be used profitably in efforts to identify gifted children from all backgrounds. If test scores are interpreted as they should be, with due consideration for individual differences in children's backgrounds, the adequacy of the test session, and the idiosyncrasies of individual tests, then standard tests can be a valuable part of an identification system, even when the children tested come from widely differing backgrounds.

In general, standard tests are most useful, and least likely to be misused, when they are administered and interpreted by people who understand both the basic principles of test construction and administration and the characteristics of specific tests. It often happens, however, that people who are not knowledgeable about testing are thrust into the position of designing identification systems. There are a number of resources that can be very useful to anyone in need of a crash course in testing. *Testing the Gifted Child: An Interpretation in Lay Language* (Fortna & Boston, 1976) provides a brief and clear introduction to the basics of test interpretation. Textbooks on assessment procedures, such as Sattler's *Assessment of Children's Intelligence* (1974) include a wealth of detailed information about technical aspects of test construction, how tests should be administered, and descriptions of individual tests. A particularly valuable resource for descriptions and evaluative reviews of individual tests is Buros' *Mental Measurements Yearbook*. At this writing, the most recent edition of this standard reference is the eighth edition, published in 1978.

Tests of General Intellectual Ability

Most identification systems are based on the assumption that intellectual ability is a fairly unitary trait. Evidence against this assumption has already been suggested. However, if the standard test component of a system for identifying intellectually gifted children of preschool age had to be limited to only one measure, the best single measure would be a test of general intelligence, or IQ.

The intelligence test most commonly used with children of preschool age is the Stanford-Binet (Form L-M, Terman & Merrill, 1973). This test is popular because of its long history and documented effectiveness (see Buros, 1978, and earlier editions for reviews) and because it covers both the age and the performance ranges necessary for evaluating the ability of intellectually advanced young children. The test is designed so that it can be administered to bright children as young as two years, zero months of age, and test items range in difficulty from very simple problems to questions that are challenging to intellectually able teenagers. This test must be administered by a highly trained examiner. It takes about an hour to give the full form. Several abbreviated versions of the test are available.

On an age scale like the Stanford-Binet, a child's performance can be compared with that of older and younger children by expressing the score in terms of mental age, i.e., the age group with which the child's performance corresponds. When the concept of IQ was first used in the early years of this century, it was literally the quotient obtained by dividing a child's mental age (MA) score on the Stanford-Binet by the child's chronological age (CA) at the time of testing and multiplying the result by 100. Thus, a child who earned an MA of six years, zero months when tested at CA four years, zero months had an IQ of 150 (IQ = 6 years/4 years X 100 = 150). In recent years most IQ tests, including the Stanford-Binet, have been designed to yield an IQ based on the child's standing relative to other children of the same age. An IQ of 100 reflects the expected or average performance for a child of any given age. About two-thirds of all children tested are expected to obtain IQs between 84 and 116 on the Stanford-Binet. Scores within this range are indicative of a normal rate of intellectual development. Scores substantially above or below this range are achieved by only a small proportion of children. For example, an IQ score of 130 or greater is expected for about three out of 100 children in the United States. This IQ level has been used as a minimum criterion for entrance in some special education programs for gifted children. Some other programs require a minimum score of 125 or 135.

At the Seattle project, assessment time has been shortened by using a short form Stanford-Binet, which consists of the two-thirds of the test items that are marked by an asterisk on the test record booklet. When we rescored full-scale test records from the longitudinal study sample as if only the short form items had been given, we found that the overwhelming majority of children's scores changed only a few points. Furthermore, prediction of later short form IQ was as accurate for a sample of children who had been administered the short form at their initial test session as it was for children who had taken the long form (Shorr & McClelland, 1977). These results were consistent with findings reported by other investigators who compared short form and full form IQs (Sattler, 1974).

When the Stanford-Binet, or other intellectual ability tests, are used to select children for early entrance programs, the score of interest is usually the mental age (MA) rather than the IQ. School personnel who are concerned about a child's ability to keep up with an older group want to make sure that the child's level of intellectual functioning is comparable to, or even more advanced than, that of potential classmates. By using MA rather than IQ as the selection criterion, it is possible to evaluate candidates of different ages according to the same absolute performance criterion. One difficulty with this procedure is that, as a result of restandardization of the Stanford-Binet in 1972, the MA scores obtained no longer represent the actual age levels at which the children are functioning. For example, a child who earns a Stanford-Binet MA of six years, zero months is not working at the level of the average six-year-old in the United States today, but at the level of the average child aged five years, seven months. Revised MAs suitable for use in making grade placement decisions have been published in journal articles (Salvia, Ysseldyke, & Lee, 1975; Shorr, McClelland, & Robinson, 1977).

The principal disadvantage of the Stanford-Binet as a selection instrument is that it yields only an index of general intellectual functioning. The Binet includes many different types of problems that are thought to tap several cognitive abilities (Ramsey & Vane, 1970; Sattler, 1974), but the structure of the test does not readily permit evaluation of a child's skills in particular cognitive areas. Two other tests for young children do permit this type of interpretation.

The WPPSI (Wechsler, 1967) is a general intelligence test for children between the ages of three years, ten-and-a-half months and six years, seven-and-a-half months. The test is divided into Verbal and Performance Scales, and each scale consists of five individual subtests. These subtests have been found to measure several different types of intellectual ability (Coates & Bromberg, 1973). Subtest scores must, however, be interpreted with caution since they are less reliable than subscale or total test scores (Wechsler, 1967).

The WPPSI, like the Binet, must be administered by a highly trained examiner in a session lasting approximately one hour. The WPPSI is not popular as an instrument for identifying young children with superior intellectual abilities because of its limited range. It was not standardized for administration to two- and three-year-olds, and it does not contain sufficiently challenging items to test the limits of bright preschoolers' abilities.

Several studies have reported that children's WPPSI IQs tend to be lower than their Stanford-Binet IQs (Kaufman, 1973a; Rellas, 1969; Ruschival & Way, 1971), but these studies were based on a comparison of the WPPSI with the 1960 edition of the Stanford-Binet. IQs for young children on the 1972 revision of the Binet tend to be about 10 points lower than on the previous version, and this overall discrepancy may no longer be a problem.

Ruschival and Way (1971) found a positive correlation of only .45 between the Stanford-Binet and WPPSI IQs of 30 children, four and five years of age, whose Stanford-Binet IQs were all 120 or higher. This correlation is substantially below the .75 reported in the test manual (Wechsler, 1967) for a less able sample of 111 five- and six-year-olds. Rellas (1969) found that several subtests of the WPPSI (Block Design, Mazes, and Arithmetic) had insufficient "top," or ceiling, to permit differentiation among high-ability children at the ages of five and six. Similarly, when 11 children from the Seattle project, whose ages ranged from three years, ten months to five years, three months, were administered the WPPSI, more than half of their subtest scores were above the ceiling for the test. Although the group's mean scores on the WPPSI (140.6) and Binet (142.6) were similar, the range of scores was much narrower for the WPPSI, and scores on the two tests were not strongly correlated (Shorr & McClelland, 1977).

The problem of insufficient ceiling on WPPSI subtests can be partially overcome by continuing on to comparable subtests of the more advanced Wechsler Intelligence Scale for Children-Revised, or WISC-R, (Wechsler, 1974) whenever a child makes too few errors to establish a ceiling on a WPPSI subtest. Although the WISC-R was not standardized for use with children under the age of six years, young children's performance on sections of this test can be interpreted in terms of "test age" norms. One can say, for example, that a four-year-old's performance on the WISC-R Block Design subtest was at the level scored by the average eleven-year-old. This strategy has been used extensively in the Seattle project, and some children of preschool age have performed at extremely advanced levels on WISC-R subtests.

The McCarthy Scales of Children's Abilities (McCarthy, 1972) is another individually administered intelligence test that might be appropriate for screening young children. The McCarthy is similar in content and structure to the WPPSI, but has the advantage of being designed for a wider age range (two-and-a-half through eight years). This test has been found to yield scores that are good predictors of school performance and show substantial correspondence to scores earned on the Stanford-Binet and WPPSI (Kaufman, 1973a). Its subtests seem to measure several different types of intellectual ability (Kaufman & Hollenbeck, 1973). The staff of the Seattle project found, however, that many bright children of preschool age were unwilling to attempt several sections of the test. In our experience, the subtest most often refused was Verbal Memory, Part II, which requires a child to retell a short story that the examiner has recited. To earn a high score on the McCarthy test, a child must perform consistently well on virtually every subtest. Thus, even though the children in the Seattle sample typically earned very high scores on some subtests, their overall McCarthy IQs (the General Cognitive Index score) were much lower than both their Binet and their WPPSI IQs (Shorr & McClelland, 1977). Further research is needed to determine whether the McCarthy is an appropriate instrument for identifying intellectually gifted children of preschool age.

The Stanford-Binet, WPPSI, and McCarthy Scales are by far the most comprehensive and trusted measures of general intellectual ability suitable for administration to children of preschool age. All of them, however, share the disadvantage of requiring administration by a highly trained psychometrician. Thus, many programs cannot afford to include any of these instruments as part of their identification procedures. Several other tests have become popular identification instruments because they can be administered in a half-hour or less by a relatively untrained examiner. The best known of these quick tests are the Peabody Picture Vocabulary Test or PPVT (Dunn, 1970) and the Slosson Intelligence Test (Slosson, 1963).

The PPVT actually tests a child's knowledge of vocabulary, but the test can be scored to yield both an estimated mental age and an estimated IQ. Since the test format requires only that a child point to whichever of four pictures best illustrates a word spoken by the examiner, the PPVT is easy to administer to very young children. The test is standardized for the age range two years, six months to eighteen years. Although young children's PPVT scores tend, on the whole, to be substantially related to their scores on full-scale intelligence tests, they should not be considered interchangeable with scores from these tests. Several investigators have found that the PPVT IQs of ethnic minority and economically disadvantaged children tend to be substantially lower than their Stanford-Binet IQs (Sattler, 1974). The PPVT would not, therefore, be appropriate for use in any program that involved applicants from diverse ethnic or economic backgrounds. Furthermore, a study of 17 children from the Seattle project indicated that the correspondence between PPVT and Stanford-Binet IQs was minimal (.27) for children with Binet IQs above the median for the group, although the relationship between the two test scores was quite strong (.83) for children with more modest Binet scores (Shorr & McClelland, 1977).

Group tests of general intellectual ability are never appropriate for use with children of preschool age. Few preschool children are sufficiently attentive, compliant, and persistent to demonstrate advanced intellectual ability in a group testing situation.

Tests of Specific Intellectual and Academic Ability

In the 1920s when Terman began his longitudinal study of gifted children, most psychologists agreed that individual differences in intellectual ability could best be described in terms of a single, general factor, sometimes called g. Although g is still considered a good index of individual differences, many psychologists have adopted a conception of intellectual functioning that includes consideration of two or three particular types of intellectual ability, which show only a moderate degree of correspondence within any individual. According to Horn (1976), some researchers have identified verbal comprehension, induction, number, and spatial orientation factors in children's test performance, while others have distinguished between items involving auditory and visual input, or between performance on verbal and nonverbal tasks. Short-term memory ability has often been reported to be relatively independent of other forms of intellectual ability, but this position has recently been criticized (Bachelder & Denny, 1977). Some theorists have argued that intellectual performance is fairly unitary at pre-school age and becomes progressively differentiated throughout childhood (Thompson & Grusec, 1970). Specific factors have, however, been identified in the test performance of very young children (Coates & Bromberg, 1973; McCall, Hogarty, & Hurlbut, 1972; Meyers et al, 1962).

The Seattle project has adopted the hypothesis that specific intellectual abilities may well exist in any cross-section of preschool-aged children and that these abilities may be more apparent in the test performance and everyday behavior of intellectually advanced children than in the performance and behavior of average ability children.

Even if intellectual abilities in children of preschool age were to prove not to be independent, there are practical reasons for designing an identification system to include several different measures of intellectual ability. Very young children are rarely so consistently cooperative that they can be relied upon to demonstrate the best performance of which they are capable during all phases of a test session. If a session contains several measures that can be evaluated separately, one's chances of observing evidence of a child's advanced capabilities are greatly increased. Our testing philosophy has been that the most meaningful aspect of a young child's test performance is not the child's average level of performance across a wide range of tasks, but the most advanced performance demonstrated. This is admittedly an unconventional view. A basic tenet of psychometric theory is the principle that performance on a composite measure, such as an IQ, is more reliable and meaningful than performance on components of that total score. The validity of the position we advocate remains to be proven, but our experience to date has given us increasing confidence in the view that a three-year-old who reads fluently but earns a Stanford-Binet IQ of only 120, or who performs like a seven-year-old on tests of spatial reasoning ability but is only moderately advanced in other skills, is a very different child from a three-year-old whose performance is consistently, but never extremely, advanced.

Consider the case of a boy we shall call Bruce. When Bruce first visited the Seattle project a few days before his third birthday, he was a less than ideally cooperative subject for standard testing. He earned a Stanford-Binet IQ of 126 with test behavior rated "detrimental" by the examiner. He would not respond to any questions requiring more than a single word answer and was generally ill at ease in the testing situation. During this same session, however, he gave an informal demonstration of his extraordinarily advanced reading skill by sounding out words such as "buttercup" from a book that was in the testing room. Bruce's command of written language was also apparent in samples of his artwork that his mother had brought to the testing session. Bruce incorporated words and numbers in his drawings, labelling a car "BUICK" and placing it near a sign that said "PARK."

Three months later, after he had enrolled in the Seattle project's Child Development Preschool, Bruce earned another disappointingly modest IQ—a General Cognitive Index of 116 on the McCarthy Scales. This time his test behavior was rated "good."

At the age of three, instances of Bruce's "best performance" on standard tests were limited to the single area of reading and writing. At the age of four, however, he earned a WPPSI IQ of 151 and was beginning to show what was to be a consistent pattern of excellence in tests involving arithmetic skill and spatial-perceptual reasoning ability as well as reading.

By the time Bruce completed his kindergarten year at the Child Development Preschool, his Stanford-Binet performance was above the limits of the published norms for the test. His reading recognition skill was at the fifth-grade level, reading comprehension at the fourth-grade level, and mathematics at the seventh-grade level.

Bruce's performance in the preschool classroom was consistent with his test performance. During his first year in the program, he did not stand out as one of the more remarkable children in the group. He was not nearly as talkative or eloquent as some of the others, and he seemed to spend an inordinate amount of time drawing pictures of cars and trucks. His reading and writing skills were readily apparent to all his teachers, but Bruce did not seem to be as broadly "gifted" as some of his classmates. By the time he was five, however, Bruce was clearly one of the most capable learners in the program. His reading skills were still progressing well, but his interests and energies seemed to have become concentrated on learning mathematics.

We could tell similar stories about the progress of other children whose "best performance" was initially on tests of spatial reasoning ability, reading, or mathematics skill. We cannot claim that these children have developed in *more* exceptional ways than children who earned very high scores on standardized intelligence tests administered at the age of two or three years, but they have certainly held their own (Robinson, Jackson, & Roedell, 1978).

The Seattle project staff translated the "best performance" philosophy into an identification battery that includes measures of spatial-perceptual reasoning skill, short-term memory, mathematics, and reading ability, as well as a measure of general intellectual ability (the starred items in the short form of the Stanford-Binet). The breadth of a child's intellectual abilities has certainly not been ignored, but selections for the special program at the Child Development Preschool have been made on the basis of excellence in specific abilities as well.

While the Stanford-Binet is a measure of general intellectual functioning, it is heavily weighted with items probing verbal knowledge and verbal reasoning ability. Measures of nonverbal, or spatial-perceptual reasoning ability, therefore provide a particularly useful complement to the Binet. We have used the Block Design and Mazes subtests of the WPPSI (Wechsler, 1967) to assess the spatial reasoning ability of children ages three years, four months through five years. These tests have been identified in previous studies as loading heavily on spatial ability in older children and adults (Eliot & Salkind, 1975; Sattler, 1974) and seem to require fewer and less advanced fine motor skills than some of the other available measures of spatial ability. Success on the Geometric Design subtest of the WPPSI, for instance, requires a degree of drawing skill that is beyond the sensorimotor coordination of most three-year-old children.

We compensate for the limited range of the Block Design or the Mazes subtests of the WPPSI by using somewhat unorthodox techniques. Although the WPPSI has not been standardized for children younger than three years, ten months, we have found that children as young as three years, four months can sometimes perform capably on the Block Design and Mazes subtests. To interpret the performance of this youngest group, we have extrapolated downward from the published norms. As noted, when children complete the WPPSI subtests without making sufficient errors to establish a ceiling, the examiner continues on to the comparable subtest of the more advanced WISC-R (Wechsler, 1974). Young children's performance on subtests of this measure can be described in terms of "test age."

Although administration of tests not standardized for a particular age group understandably horrifies some psychometricians, this technique provides a useful, and often vitally necessary, tool for differentiating the performance of children whose abilities are not typical of their age group. The value of these unorthodox procedures is illustrated by the test performance record of a girl who was three years, seven months of age at the time she was tested as an applicant for the Child Development Preschool. Although this child was officially too young to be administered the WPPSI, she earned credit for the most advanced items on the WPPSI Block Design and for some WISC-R items to earn a "test age" of seven years, ten months. To date, the most extremely advanced spatial reasoning performance recorded at the Seattle project was that of a five-year-old boy who earned a WISC-R Block Design score above the norm for 16-year-olds.

Several years' experience with the use of the Block Design and Mazes tasks to identify advanced spatial reasoning ability in children of preschool age has established that these measures yield reliable scores. When the test performance of the Child Development Preschool children in the fall of 1976 was compared with their performance in the spring of 1977, the test-retest correlation (Spearman rho) of WPPSI Mazes scores for 18 children was .71 (p<.01) and that of Block Design scores for 19 children was .65 (p<.01). Given the age of the children and the period of time between tests, these figures compare favorably with figures for the stability of more comprehensive measures. As an index of comparison, it is worth noting that the fall-to-spring test-retest reliability for the short form Binet IQs for 35 children in this preschool group was .67.

The Block Design and Mazes subtests have also contributed information about children's abilities that is largely independent of the information gained from their Stanford-Binet IQs. In three successive samples of preschool applicants (Jackson & Robinson, 1977), Block Design-Binet correlations (Spearman rho) ranged from .27 to .38 with a median value of .37, and Mazes-Binet correlations ranged from .05 to .29 with a median value of 15. Since the Block Design and Mazes are supposed to measure closely related abilities, we anticipated that scores on these two tests would correlate closely with one another, even though they were independent of Binet scores. The correlations were not as high as expected (range .33 to .80; median .47). While this lack of correspondence between the two spatial reasoning tasks is disturbing from a theoretical standpoint, it emphasizes the practical value of including as many measures as possible in any identification battery designed for use with young children.

Although the Block Design and Mazes are good measures for three-and-a-half- to five-year-old children, these tasks are too sophisticated and require too precise motor skills to be appropriate for use with the very youngest preschool applicants. In 1978 we began using the Seguin Form Board (Stutsman, 1931; 1949) to estimate the spatial reasoning ability of two- and three-year-olds. Although the norms for this test are out of date and probably inappropriate for evaluating the performance of gifted preschoolers, the test may prove to be a useful tool for comparing children within a sample. We have found that both speed and the number of errors made in completing this geometric puzzle differentiate among very young children. The Form Board takes only about five minutes to administer, and it provides an excellent rapport-building activity for the beginning of a test session. The validity of this instrument for identifying children gifted in spatial reasoning ability remains to be determined, but the test has been classified as a measure of this ability in other populations (Maccoby & Jacklin, 1974).

A test of auditory short-term memory, the classic digit-span test, is also part of the Seattle project's screening battery. The task we have used is the Numerical Memory subtest of the McCarthy Scales (McCarthy, 1972). While an occasional child has qualified for the program on the basis of exceptionally advanced memory performance, the test has generally proved less useful than the tests of spatial reasoning ability. A major problem has been the test's unreliability. Anxiety or inattentiveness can have profound effects on a young child's performance on this type of task, and our data indicate that there may be little correspondence between a child's digit-span performance at one session and performance at another session a few months later. Six-month test-retest reliability for 28 children from our project was only .35 (Spearman rho, $p < .05$) for scores on the forward digits series. Scores for 13 children who passed some items on the backward series were even less reliable (rho = .13).

In general, the performances of the children in the longitudinal study sample on tests of memory have tended to be less advanced than their performances on other measures. For example, the mean forward digits score of a group of 28 three- and four-year-old children from the Seattle study was less than one standard deviation above the mean of the standardization sample, while mean IQ for the group was 138 (more than two standard deviations above the mean).

Nonetheless, there have been striking exceptions to this pattern. Bruce, for example, was able to repeat a forward series of seven digits and a reversed series of six digits when tested a few days after his sixth birthday.

Despite the unreliability and uncertain validity of measures of short-term memory, we continue to be interested in studying the possible long-term predictive significance of performance in this area. When children do demonstrate excellence in this type of ability, it may indicate a superior capacity to absorb new experiences (Bachelder & Denny, 1977).

Children are typically selected for preschool and kindergarten programs for the gifted on the basis of intellectual skill measures, such as the general and specific ability tests just described. The possibility of identifying young children for such programs on the basis of their skills in the academic areas of reading and mathematics is often overlooked. There is, however, abundant evidence that some children of preschool age have remarkably advanced academic skills.

Data from several studies of children selected for high IQ indicate that a large proportion of these children attain some reading skill before entering school (Humes & Eberhardt, 1977; Kincaid, 1969; Terman & Oden, 1947). According to reports from parents, more than 18 percent of the children in Terman's sample began reading before the age of five. About 5 ½ percent were reported to have been reading before the age of four. The proportion of early readers was about two-and-a-half times this great among the children with the very highest (170 or above) IQs (Terman & Oden, 1947). In a more recent study of sixth graders with Stanford-Binet IQs above 150 (Kincaid, 1969), parents' retrospective reports indicated that the children began reading at a mean age of four-and-a-half years. A few children in this study were reported to have started reading at the age of two. In a survey of 630 kindergarteners from a middle-class suburban district, 34 percent of the parent-nominated children evaluated as gifted were able to read prior to entering kindergarten (Humes & Eberhardt, 1977). As of September 1978, 6 of the 18 children in the Seattle project's sample of children with IQs above 164 were reading at extraordinarily advanced levels (at the norm for children twice their age).

If advanced reading skills were observed only in children who simultaneously earned high scores on tests of intellectual ability, assessment of reading skill would not need to be part of an identification system. The early readers would be identified as gifted by other means. There are, however, many young children whose "best performance" is demonstrated in reading, but not on other tests. Dolores Durkin's 1966 sample of 30 early-reading first graders in New York City included children whose Stanford-Binet IQs ranged from 82 to 170. Many of the children in her group would never have been identified for a gifted program on the basis of their intelligence test performance. Our own findings have been similar. As of September 1978, the Stanford-Binet IQs of the 18 young children within the Seattle project's longitudinal study sample who were reading at extraordinarily advanced levels ranged from 96 to above the scale limits.

One reason that reading skill is often overlooked in the identification of gifted children is the feeling of some educators that advanced reading ability is not a good indicator of more general intellectual and academic excellence. The long-term predictive significance of early reading has not been firmly established, and it certainly cannot be claimed that all precocious readers will ultimately develop the broad range of exceptional skills we have seen in Bruce and a few other children in our sample. All the available data are, nonetheless, consistent with the hypothesis that children who begin reading at an unusually early age are likely to be good students in later years (Durkin, 1966) and that early readers tend to be highly represented in groups of very bright children (Kincaid, 1969; Terman & Oden, 1947). Moreover, reading is an ability worth nurturing in its own right. Even if a child's giftedness is limited to reading, diagnosis of his or her skill level will permit the design of a program appropriate to that child's needs.

Reading is an easy ability to measure in young children. Those who can read are usually willing to display their skill in some manner or another. A small assortment of books with large type can be used to get an informal estimate of reading ability. If a slightly more standardized assessment is desired, a single sheet of paper printed with capital and lower case letters, and words and sentences of varied difficulty, can be used as part of a testing battery. The Seattle project has used an assessment instrument of this type designed by a project staff member (McClelland, 1977) as part of the preschool identification process. Examiners have noted which words or letters a child reads correctly and tried to observe whether a child was making reasonable, if sometimes incorrect, attempts to sound out unfamiliar words. If a child was reluctant to read aloud, the examiner read from various parts of the page and asked the child to point to the words being read.

There are, unfortunately, no formal tests of reading skill that are standardized for children of preschool age. Reading readiness tests designed for this age group are simply not appropriate for assessing advanced reading skills. Such tests are not designed to identify a child who is already reading, much less differentiate one who is reading at the fourth-grade level. Furthermore, a precocious reader will not necessarily perform well on reading readiness tests (Torrey, 1969).

At the Seattle project, however, we have found that an academic achievement test designed for school-aged children can be used effectively to assess the reading and mathematics skill levels of children as young as three. The Peabody Individual Achievement Test, or PIAT, (Dunn & Markwardt, 1970) is easy to administer to preschool-aged children; its subtests start at sufficiently low pre-academic levels to permit virtually any bright child, reader or nonreader, to have some successes; and it can be administered in a half-hour or less by an examiner who needs only a few training sessions.

The PIAT can be a useful instrument for identification, diagnosis, and program evaluation. Children's scores on the two reading subtests (Reading Recognition and Reading Comprehension) and the Mathematics subtest have proven to be reliable and to discriminate effectively among children. As one would expect, four-year-olds tend to earn higher scores than three-year-olds, and children selected for a gifted program earn higher scores than unselected children from comparable backgrounds. For gifted preschool children, performance on the reading subtests has been found to be relatively independent of Stanford-Binet IQ, but performance on the Mathematics and General Information subtests has been strongly correlated with IQ (Shorr, Jackson, & Robinson, in press).

Although mathematics, like reading, is usually thought of as an academic skill area rather than a basic intellectual ability, tests of mathematical ability are included on tests of intelligence designed for preschool children. The Stanford-Binet, WPPSI, and McCarthy Scales all include counting and computation problems. It is, therefore, possible to estimate young children's mathematical ability from any of several instruments. A combination of mathematics items from the Stanford-Binet and the Arithmetic subtest of the WPPSI is used at the Seattle project to estimate the mathematical ability of preschool applicants. While this procedure is fairly economical in terms of time, it does not provide sufficient challenge for children who are exceptionally precocious in mathematics (Rellas, 1969). When a more extensive assessment of a child's mathematics skills is called for, the Mathematics subtest of the PIAT is appropriate. A more comprehensive profile of mathematics skills can be obtained from the KeyMath Diagnostic Arithmetic Test (Connolly, Nachtman, & Pritchett, 1976). This test, like the PIAT, is presented in a multiple-choice format that is easy to administer to young children, and its subtest structure permits evaluation of a child's skills in such areas as numeration, computation, money, and measurement. When the KeyMath and PIAT mathematics scores of 15 three- and four-year-olds in the

Seattle project were compared, the correlation was .74 (Spearman rho), and the group's mean performance level was similar on both measures—late kindergarten level for the PIAT and beginning first grade for the KeyMath.

Another approach to the identification of mathematical ability in young children is the assessment of their understanding of the logical principles that underlie the number system and its use in computation. Children's comprehension of the principles of seriation, class inclusion, and invariance of quantity (conservation) is related to their readiness to master mathematical skills. (See Jackson, Robinson, & Dale, 1977, for a review of this literature.) Tests of these abilities have not been designed to meet the same technical standards as the more traditional psychometric instruments, but formal or informal assessment of children's logical reasoning skills might be a useful component of an identification system.

Goldschmidt and Bentler (1968) have developed a set of materials for the standardized administration of Piaget's tests of conservation abilities. Their Concept Assessment Kit (CAK) provides three forms of a sequence of conservation measures. Norms are provided for the mean performance of children aged four through eight years. When Form A of the CAK was administered to 19 three- and four-year-olds in the Seattle project, 12 showed some evidence of conservation. Performance was moderately related to chronological age, Binet Mental Age, PIAT Reading Recognition and Total scores, and Block Design scores (Krinsky et al., 1977). The retesting of 12 of these children indicated that most bright children make substantial gains in conservation performance during their kindergarten year.

Testing Young Children's Productive Thinking Ability

The U.S. Office of Education (1972) has specified "creative or productive thinking" ability as one of the areas of giftedness for which special programs should be designed. The federal law does not, however, adequately address the very serious problem of defining and measuring this type of giftedness.

When the layman or the legislator thinks about creativity, what comes to mind is the production of unusual and socially valuable ideas or objects. As noted, the traditional, commonsense approach to the identification of creativity has always been based on the evaluation of an individual's actual creative work —an artist's portfolio, a musician's performance, or a scientist's theories. Authorities might differ in their value judgments about particular creative products, but there has never been much disagreement about the basic validity of this direct approach. Since the 1960's, however, there has been substantial interest in the measurement of what might be called creative potential by assessment of thought processes or personality traits that seem to characterize truly creative individuals. The practical value of this approach is especially apparent when the individuals to be evaluated are young children. The judgment of young children's creativity on the basis of their actual products is bound to be a difficult undertaking. In most areas of accomplishment, creative achievement requires a level of skill that can only be acquired with years of experience or training.

None of the measures labeled as tests of creativity is actually a direct test of real-life creativity. The same might be said of intelligence tests, but the problem is more troublesome with regard to creativity because there is little agreement as to what the tests should actually measure or predict. The ability measured by these tests is referred to here as productive thinking ability, because this is the term used by the U.S. Office of Education and because it seems adequate as a description of the kinds of behaviors called for in the various tests. Another common term for productive thinking is divergent production, as contrasted with the convergent production measures in IQ or achievement tests. This distinction is based on Guilford's (1967) Structure of Intellect model of intellectual functioning.

All the productive thinking measures differ from intelligence and achievement tests in that the problems they pose have not one, but many, correct answers. Productive thinking tests present situations that ask children to propose as many alternative solutions as possible. Children might, for example, be asked to think of all the ways a paper cup might be used, to describe sets of circumstances that might have led up to a scene portrayed in a drawing, or to decorate each of a set of circles with a different pattern. Responses may be judged simply on the basis of quantity (fluency) or some consideration may be given to their unusualness (originality or uniqueness) or to the child's ability to shift gears and produce responses that differ substantially from one another. Responses that clearly fail to fit the requirements of the task are usually not given credit, but stringent standards of quality are not imposed.

The rationale behind the use of productive thinking measures as predictors of creative potential has been summarized by Crockenberg (1972):

A number of distinguished people from the arts and sciences have mentioned the free flow of ideas as a crucial stage in the creative process; therefore, it is reasonable for psychologists interested in creative process to use the production of ideas as a measure of this process. (p. 40)

This is, of course, essentially an assertion that the tests have face validity. The processes measured in tests of productive thinking are said to be important processes in and of themselves. The evidence on this point has been discussed in several review articles (Horn, 1976; Wallach, 1970). A summary of this literature is given in the manual for a test designed by the Educational Testing Service:

In addition to its possible ties to creative production in adulthood, divergent thinking in children is of interest in its own right. Originality, spontaneity, and flexibility in thinking are all desirable in and of themselves. Moreover, studies by Getzels and Jackson (1962), Torrance (1963), Wallach and Kogan (1965), and others have suggested links between the cognitive aspects of divergent thinking abilities and desirable personality characteristics in children. For example, the individual high in divergent thinking has been seen as more sensitive, more open to experience, and more willing to take chances in interpersonal as well as cognitive contexts.

Many cautions are necessary in interpreting this work. Research in divergent thinking has been far less systematic than that concerning the convergent thinking abilities, and researchers have tended to be overwilling to generalize their findings to tasks and populations other than those with which they have worked. Changes in the implications of divergent thinking as the child develops, the stability of divergent thinking abilities over time, interrelationships of various divergent thinking measures at any given time—all these areas are ones in which there is more supposition than knowledge.

Given these uncertainties, care should be taken against overstating the implications of performance on tests of divergent thinking. . . . Children who are high on divergent thinking should be seen as possessing a set of cognitive abilities distinct from those assessed by standard indicators, which deserve to be esteemed and encouraged in themselves; which *may* imply a greater openness and sensitivity in other areas of the child's present functioning; and which *may* more distantly affect the likelihood that the child will become an innovative, productive adult. (Ward, 1974–75, 1979, 298–299)

There is considerable evidence that skills measured by productive thinking tests are substantially independent of skills measured by intelligence tests, although there is a positive relationship between the two types of abilities. The independence of the two areas of ability has been demonstrated in children of all ages from kindergarten students to adults (Gallagher & Crowder, 1957; Horn, 1976; Wallach, 1970). The independence of productive thinking scores and IQs tends to be greater in individuals with above-average IQs. Productive thinking ability as measured by verbal responses is relatively independent of productive thinking as demonstrated in tasks calling for drawing skill, indicating that there may be be more than one type of productive thinking ability (Horn, 1976; Wallach, 1970).

There has been some suggestion that measures of young children's productive thinking ability may predict qualities of their classroom behavior that are not predicted by intelligence tests. Singer and Whitton (1971) found that a verbal measure of productive thinking predicted the degree of facial expressiveness and depiction of motion in figure drawings by kindergarten children. Singer and Rummo (1973) found relationships between kindergarten children's productive thinking scores and some aspects of teachers' ratings of their style of play; these relationships were more extensive for boys than for girls. While findings such as these are interesting, they do not provide an adequate definition of what it is that productive thinking tests measure in young children.

Part of the difficulty in establishing even the face validity of productive thinking measures lies in the unreliability of most measures (Horn, 1976; Thorndike, 1972; Wallach, 1970). Some of this unreliability can be traced to specific aspects of the testing situation. Ward (1969) found, for instance, that the fluency of nursery school children's responses in a productive thinking task was influenced by the setting in which the task was administered. The setting had little effect on low-scoring children, but the high scorers greatly increased their production of responses when tested in a room that was rich in objects they could use for answers. Another factor that may contribute to the unreliability of productive thinking scores is the possible sensitivity of these scores to the child's feeling of ease in the testing situation. Shyness, anxiety about producing a great number of responses in a limited time, and concern that responses might not be acceptable could all have substantial effects on children's performance (Crockenberg, 1972).

Productive thinking measures designed expressly for children of preschool age are rare and relatively untried. However, measures designed for use with older children may be appropriate for some preschool children. The Wallach and Kogan Creativity Battery (1965) for children of kindergarten and elementary school age includes several tasks that call for children to generate verbal responses. These responses are scored for fluency and uniqueness. This battery has an apparent advantage over some other measures in that the ten scores obtained (fluency and uniqueness measures for each of five subtests) are substantially intercorrelated (Crockenberg, 1972). The Wallach and Kogan battery was designed as a research instrument rather than a standard test, and its use has been primarily restricted to research situations. The measures might be used, however, as a source of ideas for informal evaluation procedures.

The Torrance Tests of Creative Thinking (1966; 1974) are commercially available and have been used in many applied contexts, including identification of gifted children for special programs. Although designed for kindergarteners through graduate students, the tasks might be suitable for use with some four-year-olds. The tests are divided into sections measuring verbal and figural productive thinking ability. The verbal portion is scored for fluency, flexibility, and originality of responses, and the figural portion for fluency, flexibility, originality, and elaboration. Reviewers of the 1966 version of this test battery have been less than enthusiastic. Test-retest reliability has not been within acceptable ranges, particularly for the figural portion of the test (Crockenberg, 1972). Evidence for the unity of the individual subscores has been weak. According to Wallach (1970, p. 1232), it has not been possible "to find evidence suggesting that the Torrance instruments cohere among themselves to a degree greater than that to which they correlate with tests of convergent thinking." There is also substantial concern as to whether the battery is a valid predictor of creativity, or even a more limited sort of fluency or originality, in everyday behavior

(Crockenberg, 1972; Thorndike, 1972; Wallach, 1970). The tests are popular, nonetheless. Torrance has developed a preliminary version of a creativity battery for preschoolers called Thinking Creatively in Action and Movement (Torrance, 1974).

Another productive thinking test for young children is the Make-A-Tree subtest of the Educational Testing Service's CIRCUS battery (Ward, 1974–75, 1979). This battery was designed to provide indices of children's readiness for school in several different cognitive areas. It was standardized for five- and six-year-olds. All the other sections of the CIRCUS battery fall within the general realm of intelligence or achievement tests, but the Make-A-Tree was designed to be a test of figural productive ability. Children are given a pile of colored stickers and asked to make a picture of a tree. A week later they are asked to repeat the task, making a tree as different as possible from their first product. Children's productions are judged according to their Appropriateness (representational quality), Unusualness, and Difference (between the first and second tree).

The Make-A-Tree instrument was not intended as a device to be used in identifying gifted children, and its suitability for that purpose has yet to be established. The results of a preliminary study at the Seattle project suggest, however, that this test may have some potential as an identification tool (McClelland, 1977b). Make-A-Tree was administered to 25 children in the age range from three through five years who were attending the Child Development Preschool. The children enjoyed the task, although some had difficulty manipulating the gummed stickers. Their products could be rated reliably by two independent raters using the standards supplied in the test manual. The older children in the group earned higher scores than the younger children. The performance of the group as a whole was significantly better than that of the norming sample on two of the three subscales (Unusualness and Difference). The Make-A-Tree scores were not related to the children's scores on any of three tests of intellectual ability—the Stanford-Binet, WPPSI Block Design, or WPPSI Mazes.

Make-A-Tree has some face validity as a measure of young children's productive thinking in the realm of graphic production. It is comparatively well normed, fun to administer, and easy to score. Our limited data suggest that it is capable of differentiating among high ability children and that it yields information that is not redundant with the information that can be gained from traditional tests of intellectual ability. Unfortunately, we are not aware of any data that indicate that children's Make-A-Tree performance is reliable, a valid indicator of any important aspect of their everyday behavior at time of testing, or related to behaviors or characteristics that are stable over time.

Another approach to the study of young children's creativity is illustrated by Starkweather's (1971) research battery of four scales, which includes form board and color preference tests designed to measure conforming and nonconforming behavior, a target game intended to measure children's willingness to try difficult tasks, and an originality test that asks the child to name shapes constructed of plastic foam. Starkweather's conception of creativity is quite different from that of Wallach and Kogan or Torrance. She is less concerned with specific aspects of productive thinking than in measuring a broad spectrum of qualities that might be evident in a highly creative child (1964; 1971). Starkweather's measures provide potentially interesting research tools, but are not appropriate for use as standard tests of creativity or productive thinking.

Despite the limitations inherent in all the available measures of productive thinking, these measures are, and will probably continue to be, widely used as tools for identification of gifted children. One reason for their popularity is undoubtedly the body of evidence indicating that productive thinking measures yield scores that are less consistently related to socioeconomic level and ethnic group differences than are IQ and achievement measures. Some studies have found productive thinking scores to be totally unrelated to these background variables, while other studies have suggested an advantage for children from low-income backgrounds or certain minority groups (Torrance, 1971; Williams, Teubner, & Harlow, 1973). Children from middle-class families do tend to earn higher scores on the CIRCUS Make-A-Tree (Ward, 1974–75, 1979). Renzulli (1973) has proposed that productive thinking measures offer opportunities for minority children to respond to test items in terms unique to their own culture, rather than being constrained to produce responses defined by white, middle-class standards. Certainly this is an advantage worth considering.

The technical and conceptual weaknesses of the productive thinking measures do, however, limit their usefulness. Anyone incorporating these measures in a screening process must be scrupulously careful to consider the factors that might contribute to the substantial unreliability of the tests, such as the emotional atmosphere and time limits of the session, the availability of inspirational cues in the testing room, and so on. The evidence is consistent in indicating that verbal and figural productive thinking tests yield substantially independent scores; it is ambiguous regarding the interrelationships of such measures as fluency and originality within the verbal and figural dimensions. There is, therefore, no justification for the hope that a single measure is likely to pick out children with the full constellation of skills that provide our commonsense definition of real-life creativity (Horn, 1976; Lovell & Shields, 1967). Furthermore, the ambiguity surrounding the predictive validity of even the best measures of productive thinking raises serious doubts about how test results should be interpreted. What, precisely, should be expected of children who have qualified for a special program on the basis of high scores on some measure of productive thinking?

Perhaps the issue of predictive validity might best be circumvented by considering the quality of the child's responses, rather than simply scoring the number or uniqueness of the answers given (Crockenberg, 1972). Sisk (1977) has suggested ways in which the tasks included in productive thinking tests can be used to get an informal estimate of a young child's ability to verbalize freely and creatively about interesting situations. Similarly, the manual for the Make-A-Tree tests gives guidelines for making an interpretive diagnosis of the child's performance (Ward, 1974–75, 1979). By employing productive thinking tasks as stimuli to engage a child's interest and inspire verbal or pictorial responses that need not be limited to a predefined "correct answer," the sensitive examiner may gain meaningful insights into a child's capabilities that are, indeed, quite different from those revealed by intelligence tests.

Testing Handicapped Preschoolers

Interpreting the standard test performance of young children with physical, socio-emotional, or mental handicaps is even more difficult than interpreting the performance of young children in general. It is often necessary to adapt the administration of a test to circumvent the limitations of a child's handicap, and any adaptation makes the interpretation of the test according to standard norms questionable. Even when a test can be given to a handicapped child in its standard form, the meaning of the child's performance may be difficult to interpret. It is possible that a child's handicap has made the testing situation itself more stressful, limited the child's ability to perceive test item content or instructions or to make the required physical responses, or reduced the child's prior exposure to experiences that would have contributed to knowledge of the test content. Therefore, a handicapped child who earns the same score as a non-handicapped child may actually be demonstrating a more unusual performance and greater capacity for future learning.

Because of the problems inherent in the administration of standard tests to handicapped children, programs for handicapped gifted children often focus on identification by teacher and parent nomination techniques. Identification procedures can also involve some form of standard test assessment, tailored to the child's limitations and suspected strengths (Blacher-Dixon, 1977; Hanninen 1978; Karnes & Bertschi, 1978).

Staff members of Connecticut's Project SEARCH for gifted and talented handicapped students have developed an approach to assessment that is based on thorough knowledge of available identification instruments and sensitivity to the special issues involved in identifying the areas of cognitive strength these children may have. The Project SEARCH philosophy reflects the same "best performance" principle that we advocate for interpreting the test performance of all young children. Hokanson and Jospe (1976) suggest that:

It is necessary to study as many specific individual areas of functioning as possible and to look for splinter strengths in these areas as well as patterns of abilities which would reveal a more generalized area of superiority (a clustering) . . . with exceptional children, more so than with nonexceptional children . . . *average measures must be avoided at all costs.* (p. 5)

Hokanson and Jospe suggest particular measures likely to be appropriate for use with hearing impaired, physically handicapped, and learning disabled children, and for children with mild or severe social and emotional disorders. They discuss the importance of interpreting test results in the context of a full clinical assessment of the child's performance and of gathering comprehensive information about the child's everyday behavior and developmental history from everyone who knows the child well. When test results are used in this context, the limitations of a necessarily nonstandard administration are minimized. A similarly comprehensive approach has been used in other programs for gifted handicapped preschoolers (Karnes, 1977).

The primary limitation of the procedures advocated by Hokanson and Jospe applies to any thorough assessment of gifted handicapped children: the assessment is a time-consuming and expensive process that must involve highly trained professionals. Other authorities also stress the importance of observing a handicapped child for a considerable length of time to make the best possible judgment about the nature and degree of the child's gifts or talents (Blacher-Dixon, 1977; Karnes, 1977; Karnes & Bertschi, 1978).

Summary

Any attempt to identify excellence in young children's intellectual, academic, or productive thinking skills on the basis of their standard test performance should meet several minimal criteria:

1. The instruments used should provide reliable and valid estimates of the abilities in question.
2. Tests used to identify gifted children for special programs must be sufficiently challenging to permit children who have extraordinarily advanced skills to display them. Tests designed for older children must sometimes be used to provide this challenge.
3. The failure of a child to demonstrate a particular behavior or to earn a high test score should not in itself be taken as conclusive evidence that the child lacks the competence to perform that behavior or earn that score.
4. An assessment battery should include a variety of separate measures to increase the probability of eliciting young children's "best performance."
5. The appropriateness of assessment instruments for children from bilingual or cultural minority backgrounds or for handicapped children should be carefully evaluated in terms of the goals of the particular program and the attributes and needs of each child.

6. It should be kept in mind that a child may have important intellectual, academic, or productive thinking gifts that can be demonstrated on tests specific to particular ability areas, but that are not accompanied by a high IQ.

ISSUES IN THE INTERPRETATION OF IDENTIFICATION INFORMATION

A test battery, no matter how comprehensive, provides only a limited sample of a child's behavior. That sample may not include the best performance of which a child is capable. Because young children's standard test scores are unreliable and often inaccurately estimate their true capabilities, identification systems should provide for alternate or supplementary modes of evaluation. Programs for school-aged children often rely heavily on nominations, evaluations, or checklist descriptions from the children's teachers (see, e.g., Renzulli & Smith, 1977). Information from teachers can also contribute to the identification of preschool-aged children who have already had some preschool or day care experiences. Parents, however, are the most likely sources of information about the everyday behavior of preschool-aged children.

Most evaluations of information provided by teachers and parents for the purpose of identifying gifted children have been restricted to a format in which these sources are seen only as tools for preselecting children who will probably qualify for a program on the basis of standard test performance. In the prototypical study (see, e.g., Jacobs, 1971), parents of children in several school classes will be asked to complete a questionnaire that will be used to establish a list of parent-nominated children. The teachers will be asked for similar information, yielding a list of teacher-nominated children. Individual intelligence tests will then be administered to *all* children in the classes being studied, and the accuracy of the parents' and teachers' nominations will be evaluated against children's test scores. The assumption is that the children's standard test scores provide the appropriate criterion for determining if a child is qualified for a program. The *effectiveness* of a nomination system—or how many are overlooked—is computed as the proportion of the total number of children qualifying for the program on the basis of test performance who were picked up by the nomination procedure (number correctly nominated ÷ total number qualified). Thus, an ineffective nomination system would be one that overlooked many potentially qualified children. The *efficiency* of the procedure—or how many are overrated—is the proportion of nominated children who ultimately qualify on the basis of test performance (number correctly nominated ÷ total number nominated). In an inefficient system, many of the children nominated would fail to qualify for the program. A good nomination system is, of course, both effective and efficient.

It is fairly easy to assess efficiency (the proportion overrated) simply by determining the proportion of nominees who earn scores above the cutoff on the criterion measure. This information is usually available in program records. Unbiased estimates of effectiveness (the proportion overlooked), on the other hand, are rarely obtainable from the information routinely collected in an identification process. Scores on the criterion measures are usually available only for children who have been nominated for a program or who have survived a preliminary screening process. The ultimate criterion for classifying a child as gifted is usually an individually administered intelligence test, and such tests are rarely administered to all the children in a class.

It is one thing to estimate effectiveness relative to the number of children who did qualify for a program, and quite another to make this estimate in terms of the number who *would* qualify if scores on the criterion measure were available for all children. For example, follow-up surveys in selected schools indicated that Terman's multistage process for identifying high IQ children overlooked 20 or 25 percent of the children who might have qualified for the study had the Stanford-Binet been administered to entire school populations (Terman et al., 1925).

A second problem in the interpretation of the nomination literature is the need to develop a better standard against which the validity of nominations can be judged. The assumption that a child's score on an intelligence test or any other measure is fixed and absolute in inappropriate. In reality even the most reliable test score represents a range of performance, not a fixed value. Thus, nomination effectiveness values of 20 or 50 percent not overlooked should not be judged against an ideal standard of 100 percent. Similarly efficiency values should not be judged as if 100 percent not overrated were possible (Shorr, 1978).

This point may be easier to understand if one imagines an identification system in which children were nominated for a program on the basis of one Stanford-Binet IQ and qualified for the program on the basis of a second Stanford-Binet IQ from a test administered two weeks later. Because of unreliability in the scores, all the children nominated for the program would not qualify, and some of those who qualified would not be among the group nominated.

Finally, there is the more general problem that the criterion measures might not pick children who could benefit most from the program. By assessing the classroom performance of children who have qualified for and participated in a program and determining what proportion of this group could be described as successes (Renzulli & Smith, 1977), it is possible to estimate the proportion overrated by the identification system as a whole, nominations and tests together. But again, this type of evaluation procedure yields no information regarding the proportion overlooked in the system; it is quite possible that some children who were not selected for the program could have been as successful as any of the participants.

As programs for gifted children begin to operate on a larger scale, well-designed identification research will be needed to define the effectiveness and efficiency levels of all the component procedures within complex identification systems. The ultimate validity of these identification systems as tools for selecting the children most likely to succeed in particular programs must also be established.

IDENTIFICATION BY INFORMATION FROM PARENTS

Parents are in the best possible position to act as observers and recorders of their children's behavior, although they may not always be able to interpret or evaluate what they observe. Parents see their children when they are at ease in familiar surroundings, when they are playing by themselves as well as interacting with adults or other children. Parents are, moreover, generally interested in what their own children are doing and willing to take the time to share their observations with others.

There are several ways in which parents can be asked to share information about their children's abilities. One approach is simply to ask parents whether or not they think their child is gifted, perhaps giving a few general guidelines to use in making this judgment. A second alternative is to provide parents with a checklist of characteristics thought to be typical of a gifted child and ask them to note which characteristics describe their offspring. A third possibility is to ask parents whether their child has mastered particular skills. Finally, parents may be asked to contribute anecdotal information describing their child's accomplishments and interests. Each of these approaches has its strengths and limitations.

The first approach, which might be called parent nomination, is involved to some extent in any identification procedure initiated by parents. Since parent initiation is a likely feature of any program for gifted children of preschool age, the advantages and disadvantages of parent nomination are worth keeping in mind.

The experience of the Seattle project after several years of soliciting participants for our longitudinal study has repeatedly confirmed the finding that parents exercise considerable self-selection in responding to calls for intellectually or academically gifted children. The mean performance level of each year's group (typically about 130 in Stanford-Binet IQ) was substantially above what would be expected by chance, even allowing for the generally high education level of Seattle area residents (Jackson, 1978a). This is consistent with the findings of other studies involving parent nomination of children for gifted programs (Ciha et al, 1974; Jacobs, 1971). Parents who have the opportunity to make nominations are, more often than not, fairly realistic about their children's abilities. Thus, parent nominations can provide an efficient tool for identifying gifted children.

Despite this general finding, there are differences among socioeconomic groups in parents' tendency to describe their child as "gifted." In one study of school-aged children who had earned Stanford-Binet IQs qualifying them for a gifted program, parents from lower socioeconomic neighborhoods tended to be more likely to report that they had recognized their child as gifted than were parents from upper socioeconomic neighborhoods (Cheyney, 1962). Similarly, Ciha et al. (1974) found that parents from higher status neighborhoods tended to be less effective in nominating children who would qualify for gifted programs than were parents from lower status neighborhoods. Unfortunately, neither of these studies reports any data on social class differences in the efficiency of parent nomination. One might expect that those groups that are most effective in nominating qualified candidates might also tend to be less efficient in nominating *only* qualified candidates.

In our own research, we have found that some well-educated parents from homogeneous middle-class communities tend to be unrealistically stringent in their standards of what constitutes superior intellectual performance. As one parent noted, "In our neighborhood almost every child is reading by age four." Parents are often aware of the difficulty of rating their child's behavior because of their limited experience with "typical" behavior for children that age, and they may resist making specific judgments even though they are willing to nominate their child for a gifted program.

In the early days of our longitudinal study, we asked parents to rate various aspects of their child's development on a five-point scale ranging from "below average" to "extraordinarily precocious." We abandoned this procedure after receiving numerous complaints from parents that they simply could not make such judgments. One father offered the following criticism:

If . . . you really mean to ask us how our child seems precocious, then (unless you are only interested in our potentially egotistical guessing) why don't you inform us as to what constitutes exceptional behavior? Don't you see that to ask the question in the first place *presupposes* such standards, and that answering therefore *requires* such standards, and that in turn requires us to form them—even if we don't know how?

We agreed with this parent that it was unreasonable to ask for judgments of a child's precocity without giving parents specific standards by which they could make the judgments.

The checklist approach does not require parents to evaluate their child's precocity *per se,* but it does almost always require evaluative judgments. Parents are typically asked to say whether or not their child displays a certain quality or behavior and sometimes asked to rate the incidence or intensity of the behavior along a scale. One difficulty with checklists is that some of the characteristics listed may not, in fact, differentiate gifted from nongifted children (see Chapter

2). Another problem is that the items are often so nonspecific or evaluative that the person completing the questionnaire must make difficult interpretive decisions to answer the question. A sample of items from checklists designed for parents or teachers illustrates this problem:

Has quick mastery and recall of factual information.
____Almost all the time   ____To a considerable degree
____Occasionally   ____Seldom or never
(Borland, 1978; Renzulli & Hartman, 1971)

Uses much common sense and practical knowledge in solving problems.
1 (low)   2   3   4   5   6   7   8   9 (high)
(Seattle Public Schools Horizon Questionnaire, 1978)

Does things differently in ways that make good sense, whether it's piling up blocks, setting the table, or drying the dishes. ____Yes   ____No
(Abraham, 1976)

Is your child a keen and alert observer?
____Seldom   ____Occasionally   ____Often   ____Very Often
(Malone, 1976)

What, exactly, should the standard be for saying that a child demonstrates "quick" mastery of information, "much" common sense, or "keen and alert" observation? An individual rating a group of children might be able to make comparisons along these dimensions, but we suspect that such judgments are very difficult for parents to make. One parent might, for example, decide that a daughter who could always remember the plot line of television programs but regularly forgot her mother's instructions did indeed have the "quick mastery and recall" specified in the first question above; another parent might decide that a child with this contradictory behavior pattern did not possess the quality described. Some parents might be more likely than others to resolve these dilemmas in ways that would cause their child to appear more "gifted," particularly if a place in a desired program were at stake.

The adequacy of the checklist approach could easily be evaluated, but we know of no studies that have adequately validated the reliability, effectiveness, and efficiency of any of the available checklists designed for parents or teachers of preschool- or kindergarten-aged children. Malone and Moonan (1975) have demonstrated, in a post hoc analysis, that small sets of items from Malone's checklist could be used to differentiate kindergarten children who had qualified for a gifted program (IQ above 132) from those who had not. The sets of differentiating items were different for boys and girls. This potential relationship between test performance and characteristics reported by parents must be tested using a new sample before any claims for its validity can be made.

Our own approach in designing a parent questionnaire as part of the identification system for the Child Development Preschool and our longitudinal study was to focus on questions that were as specific and noninterpretive as we could possibly make them. We asked questions about behaviors that were directly relevant to the content and goals of our program and that were likely to be displayed in a child's everyday activities at home. Our approach is similar to one that has been used with some success in parent interview and questionnaire instruments designed to identify children with developmental problems (Alpern & Boll, 1972). Our questionnaire focuses on intellectual and academic abilities that might be displayed by gifted children two through five years of age. The following examples indicate the style and content of the items:

Has your child drawn a person with at least some representation of legs or head and eyes?

Does your child recognize and correctly identify the numbers 1 through 9?

Does your child comment on words that have two or more meanings?

Does your child read, not just listen to, books such as *Winnie the Pooh* or *Little House on the Prairie,* which contain long stories and few pictures? Examples of sentences found in these books are: "He split each log straight down the middle." and "Nothing had ever been so tempting as that watermelon on that hot day."

This questionnaire has been revised several times. Certain questions have proven very difficult to phrase in a way that will not be misinterpreted. For instance, the last question above, which was meant to refer to a very advanced level of reading skill, was sometimes answered in the affirmative by parents who indicated elsewhere in the questionnaire that their child could not read simple kindergarten-level books such as *Hop on Pop.* Some of these parents made comments that revealed they were ignoring the phrase "not just listen to." Part of the problem with this particular question might have been that some parents found it difficult to imagine preschool-aged children actually reading such books.

Despite the problems that remain, our project staff has been able to establish several points essential to the validation of the instrument. For example, an analysis of the 1978 version (Krinsky, 1978) revealed that on the average, older children earned higher scores than younger children and that there was a broad range of performance within each age group. Thirty parents completed the questionnaire on two occasions several months apart to give an estimate of the reliability of parents' responses. On the average, parents gave identical answers to 77 percent of the items, and answers differing by only one point along a four-point scale for 92 percent of the items. More than half of 30 parents questioned about procedures used in completing the questionnaire reported that they had consulted records of their child's development or asked the child to demonstrate particular skills to answer some of the questions.

Some of the questionnaire items formed logical scales of difficulty, such that a child could not reasonably be expected to possess one skill without also having mastered another. The elementary and advanced reading items mentioned above were part of one such scale, a progression of prereading and reading items. Another scale was composed of items related to mathematics skills. In general, parents' responses to items that could be ordered in this way were consistent with our expectations regarding relative difficulty. Since the questions were presented in random order, this test of "scalability" supplemented the measures of age differences and reliability in indicating that the questionnaire yielded valid information about children's abilities (Krinsky, 1978).

One limitation of the objective questionnaire approach is that is necessarily overlooks the possibility that some gifted children may be most remarkable not for what they do, but for how they do it. Another problem is that an instrument of reasonable length cannot be comprehensive enough to include all the behaviors by which a child might display exceptional talent. One way of overcoming these limitations is to supplement an objective questionnaire with an open-ended questionnaire or interview designed to collect parents' anecdotal comments regarding their child's abilities, interests, and personal style. The unstructured approach is often successful in eliciting remarks that give a vivid picture of a child's behavior.

One parent, for example, wrote the following description of her daughter's accomplishments in a letter volunteering to participate in our longitudinal study:

By the age of two, Alice could identify all colors, including shades, could count to ten, had begun "spelling" road signs by naming the letters, could identify all letters of the alphabet by name, and spoke in sentences of up to ten words, using all basic parts of speech. She now (at 28 months) speaks in sentences of up to 16 words and uses complex sentence structures; for example, this morning she has said, "I'm trying to figure out where I left my dancing shoes," and, "I want to take a look at this story to see what kinds of boys and girls it has in it." . . . Alice has memorized most of *Birds: A Guide to the Most Familiar American Birds* and recognizes the common ones we see frequently; at the zoo she identified the kingfisher, bald eagle, vultures, and owls from having seen them in the book and was indignant over the lack of a purple martin and a tufted titmouse. . . . Alice got her first books when she was six months old, and they immediately became her primary interest. She now has over a hundred books and has learned most of them by heart.

The parents of a five-year-old boy, when asked what features of their child's behavior had led them to believe he might have advanced intellectual abilities, gave the following answer:

His precocious, strong interest in symbols and their manipulation has been striking; by the age of 18 months he could readily identify all upper and lower case manuscript letters; by the age of 26 months he was reading fluently many three- and four-letter phonetic words (and many longer ones) and could spell many unaided; now, at age five, language skills seem passe to him, and he is turning his attention to mathematics.

In an interview conducted when this boy was five years, nine months of age, his mother added additional details to her description of her son's accomplishments, such as the report that he had independently discovered the standard system for multiplying two-digit numbers by breaking them down into components and summing the products of the components, e.g., $17 \times 19 = (10 \times 10) + (7 \times 9) + (7 \times 10) + (9 \times 10)$. His mother commented that he preferred using this system to the tedium of memorizing multiplication tables beyond 10.

Certainly anecdotal reports from parents can be misleading. Some parents communicate little more than a general enthusiasm for their child's lively interest in learning and quickness to grasp new concepts. It is difficult to tell whether a child described in this way is truly advanced in intellectual development or simply displaying the delightful zest for learning that characterizes most children. Also parents may occasionally misinterpret a child's accomplishment as signifying a more advanced understanding than is actually present. For instance, a child who recognizes traffic signs and grocery labels may be described as "reading" even though the child's recognition skills are limited to these specific contexts. The most helpful parents are those who provide explicit detail in their descriptions of their child's behavior.

The Seattle project's parent questionnaire has, in all its versions, combined objective questions with requests for comments for anecdotal information. Combined objective and essay responses to each questionnaire have been evaluated by a team of two trained raters. The first two versions of the questionnaire were rated by graduate students and faculty members from the project staff, but the 1978 version was rated by two undergraduate psychology students. The ability of these undergraduates to make reliable judgments in evaluating 204 questionnaires was within acceptable ranges for this type of task (tau = .65, p < .001). In only 13 of the total 1330 judgments involved in these ratings did the raters disagree by more than one point on a three-point scale (Krinsky, 1978).

The relationship between parent questionnaire information and children's concurrent test performance has been analyzed using three separate samples of children. Parents within each sample completed a slightly different version of the questionnaire. In all samples there was a positive relationship between parent information measures and children's test performance. (Correlations ranged from .24 to .56.) The relationship between parent questionnaire objective scores and short form Stanford-Binet IQ tended to be stronger for children aged three years, ten months and older than for the younger children in the sample. Scores based on responses to objective questions and scores derived from ratings of anecdotal information provided comparable predictions of test performance (Krinsky, 1978; Krinsky, Jackson, & Robinson, 1977).

Given the instability of very young children's intelligence tests scores, it would hardly be reasonable to use prediction of concurrent test performance as the sole standard for evaluating the usefulness of parent information. A better standard is the extent to which parent information predicts the child's performance in later years. Information collected from parents when their children were two or three years old has, in fact, been *more* strongly related to the children's test performance years later, when they were four or five years old, than to their test performance at the time the questionnaires were completed.

IDENTIFICATION BY INFORMATION FROM TEACHERS

Since teachers work with many different children, they are potentially in a better position than parents to make judgments about how a particular child's abilities compare to those of other children of the same age. As indicated in Table 3-1, estimates of the relative efficiency and effectiveness of parents and teachers as nominators of children for gifted programs vary from study to study. The literature suggests, nonetheless, that nominations from kindergarten teachers are not likely to be as effective as parent nominations in identifying children with high IQs.

The relative effectiveness of teacher nominations can be improved by training teachers so that they can make informed judgments (Gear, 1978) or by giving teachers a structured observation schedule to guide their evaluations (Kaufman, 1973). Jacobs (1971) reported that kindergarten teachers who were not given any guidance in criteria to use for nominating gifted children overestimated the intellectual ability of "verbally adept children who were very cooperative and appeared to elicit teacher approval for their actions" (p. 141). It also seems that untrained kindergarten teachers are more likely to nominate moderately than extremely bright children (Kaufman, 1973) and that the effectiveness of teachers' nominations may vary with the social class and ethnic composition of their classes (Ciha et al., 1974). Kindergarten teachers' ratings of children's academic abilities have also been found to be higher for girls than for boys (Stevenson et al., 1976), perhaps realistically so.

Unfortunately there is no published literature assessing preschool teachers' or day care workers' ability to make appropriate nominations of gifted children for special programs. It is possible that the smaller groups and greater allowance for individuality in the typical preschool classroom might make it easier for preschool than for kindergarten teachers to observe instances of superior ability. On the other hand, the content of the typical preschool curriculum might not offer sufficient challenge to permit gifted children to display the full extent of their abilities.

Table 3-1
Efficiency and Effectiveness of Kindergarten Teachers' and
Parents' Nominations of Gifted Children

Citation	Efficiency (Number correctly nominated ÷ total number nominated)		Effectiveness (Number correctly nominated ÷ total number qualified)	
	Teachers	Parents	Teachers	Parents
Weise, Meyers & Tuel, 1975	70.0%	—	_a	—
Jacobs, 1971	4.3%	62.0%	9.5%	72.0%
Ciha, Harris, Hoffman & Potter, 1977	24.7%	14.0%	22.4%	67.0%
Humes & Eberhardt, 1977	22.0%[b]	23.4%[b]	—	—

NOTE: Only published reports have been included in this table. Unpublished doctoral dissertations by Kaufman (1973) and Ryan (1975) provide comparable data.

[a]Effectiveness of teacher nominations was 70 percent for the sample tested, but qualifying tests were administered only to children nominated by their teachers or earning high scores on a group intelligence test.

[b]This study involved a four-stage selection procedure, with teacher *or* parent nomination constituting the first step. Efficiency values indicate the number of nominees who survived the entire sequence of selection procedures.

The findings of a study conducted within the Child Development Preschool suggest that some preschool teachers can indeed be accurate judges of children's overall intellectual maturity. In the fall and spring of the 1976–77 school year, five teachers were asked to rank order all children in the group according to relative intellectual maturity. Teachers were instructed to use their own judgment in selecting the criteria to be considered in doing this task. There was little change between the fall and spring rankings. The teachers showed substantial agreement among themselves (mean $rho = .83$), and the mean of their rankings was strongly correlated with the rank order of the 24 children's Stanford-Binet mental ages ($rho = .78$). The relationship between teachers' rankings and test performance remained strong and statistically significant even when the contribution of chronological age was controlled in the analysis (Shorr, 1978). Since these teachers were better educated than many preschool teachers and were trained to be sensitive to individual children's abilities, it is possible that they were better equipped for this task than a random group of preschool teachers would be.

Information from teachers plays an especially important role in the identification of talent among handicapped preschoolers (Blacher-Dixon, 1977; Karnes,

1977). Teacher checklists that can be used to select handicapped children who are potentially talented in the areas of general intellectual ability, mathematics, reading, or science skill, creativity, social skill, artistic or musical skill, and psychomotor ability have been developed for use in the Illinois RAPYHT (Retrieval and Acceleration of Promising Young Handicapped and Talented) model program. According to the 1977 report from this project, about half of the children selected for follow-up on the basis of checklist information qualified for the program (Karnes, 1977). Qualification was determined by different criteria for different areas of talent, with the typical standard being performance one and a half standard deviations above the mean (or the top 7 percent) on standard tests or scales measuring different types of ability.

OVERVIEW: DESIGNING AN IDENTIFICATION SYSTEM

When an identification system includes several different sources of information about a child's abilities, there are a variety of ways in which the information might be organized. One technique, often used in identification systems for school-aged children, might be called the *sequential* method. The selection process is organized into a sequence of events, perhaps parent and teacher nominations, followed by group testing, and then by individual testing. Any child who fails to score above a certain cutoff on any part of the sequence is eliminated from further consideration. The rationale for this system is economic; the final stage, usually an individually administered test, is so expensive that some prior selection of candidates is required. While a sequential method of selection may be unavoidable, each stage of the process is necessarily somewhat imprecise, and the possibility of inappropriately disqualifying children is present at every stage. Another problem with the sequential model is that final selections are sometimes made *only* on the basis of a child's performance on the ultimate selection instrument, and valuable information collected during the initial stages of the process is disregarded.

Chances for giving fair consideration to every applicant are increased by relying as much as possible on a *simultaneous, or case study,* model of selection. Ideally, all applicants participate in all stages of the selection process, and all information is considered in making final selections. Renzulli and Smith (1977) have demonstrated that this model need not be unduly expensive and suggest that collection of comprehensive information may be substituted for the administration of individual tests. For children of preschool age, however, individual test sessions are necessary for identification of advanced intellectual or academic skills. Group tests, as noted, are not appropriate for this age range, and the children are unlikely to demonstrate the full range of their skills in a classroom setting. Test information can, of course, be considered jointly with information from other sources. The more varied the array of information, the more likely a system is to reveal each child's strengths.

The identification of gifted young children is no easy task, and no identification system, no matter how expensive and time consuming, will ever provide the perfect tool for selecting the best qualified applicants for a program. When constraints of time and money as well as the imperfect state of the art of identification are taken into consideration, any system will be a compromise. To make the compromise an optimal one, persons charged with responsibility for designing an identification system might find it helpful to ask themselves the following questions:

1. Does the standard test component of the identification system include measures of a child's abilities in each area relevant to the content and goals of the program?
2. Are all the measures included in the identification relevant to the program?
3. Are the standard tests known to yield reliable and valid estimates of abilities for children who are likely to perform at levels far beyond those expected for their age group?
4. Does the system include consideration of information about a child's everyday behavior collected from parents or others who know the child well?
5. Are those who are a part of the identification process trained to consider all aspects of the available information, such as the adequacy of the test session or special features of the child's background?
6. Are all components of the identification system appropriate for use with children from the cultural groups represented among the applicants?
7. Can a child qualify for the program despite a low score on an individual component of the identification battery if performance is very strong on other components?
8. Can the identification process be accomplished with the time, staff, and funds available?

The last query is, of course, the *sine qua non* of any identification system. It is worth making some compromises on identification if the economy will result in freeing needed resources for the actual operation of the program.

The process of selecting some children for a gifted program almost always involves rejecting other children, either because they do not seem to have the abilities necessary to qualify for the program or because there are simply not enough places for all qualified applicants. When informing parents that their child has not been accepted, program personnel should remember that this decision might well be the result of errors or inadequacies in the identification system rather than any actual limitations of the child.

In dealing with applicants to the Child Development Preschool, we have tried to be honest about the imperfections of our identification system, while remaining firm about the need to use some systematic basis for selections. When a child did not qualify for the program, we tied our negative decision to the fact that the child's performance at a particular time did not meet the particular requirements of our program. Parents of children who would still be of preschool age the following year were always invited to reapply.

Nothing we do can overcome entirely the disappointment of parents who hoped their child would be selected for a program, but we must do our best to keep that event from having an enduring negative effect on parents' perceptions of their child.

4

PROGRAMS
FOR GIFTED
YOUNG CHILDREN

SINCE GIFTED children are not all alike—
their vast individual differences in intellectual, physical, emotional, and social development have been documented in Chapter 2—it follows that there is no single
program that will be equally beneficial to every child identified as gifted. Different
children need different types of programs, depending on their individual profiles of
abilities and interest.

BASIC PRINCIPLES IN PROGRAM PLANNING

Specific programs will be described later, but an understanding of the
basic steps used in planning such programs is needed first.

Using the Identification System

One way to increase the chances that a program will be appropriate for
a particular group of children is to use the identification system as the major
basis for program planning (Renzulli & Hartman, 1971; Robinson, Roedell, &
Jackson, 1979). If children are selected for advanced intellectual skills, the program should offer stimulating material to challenge those skills; if children are
identified for musical talent, the program should include intensive instruction in
music, and so on.

The identification system, however, can provide only the initial clues for
the creation of programs. Whatever their particular gifts or talents, all young
children need a broadly based program designed to nurture their physical, social, and intellectual development. Even when a group of children has been
selected for a particular type of superior skill, they may differ among themselves
both in their degree of advancement and in their levels of development in other
skill areas. It is not uncommon for a gifted child to show advanced development
in one area and average or even below average development in other areas. An
effective program will provide individualized activities that build on and challenge children's strengths while allowing for guided development in areas of

The principal author of this chapter is Wendy Conklin Roedell.

weakness. Sometimes teachers may focus too much attention on children's weaknesses to the exclusion of their strengths. A tendency to teach to the lowest level of a child's ability is as unfortunate as a tendency to nurture only the child's strong areas.

The Value of Observation

To plan individualized programs, a teacher must become an accurate observer of children's behavior. One good introduction to classroom observation is *The Classroom Observer* by Ann Boehm and Richard Weinberg (1977). Staff of the Child Development Preschool have developed an informal observation guide to help teachers expand their awareness of the many different ways children may display advanced abilities in the classroom. The following list of "things to notice about children's behavior" is far from comprehensive, but can serve as a starting point for refining observation skills.

1. Notice when a child uses advanced vocabulary correctly or when a child asks about a new word heard in a story or lesson and then practices that word.
2. Notice when a child uses metaphors or analogies. For example, a child might say that moss on a tree is like an old man's beard, thus going beyond the simple perception of moss.
3. Notice when a child spontaneously makes up songs or stories, particularly when these elaborate on new experiences or when they involve "playing" with the pronunciation of words, rhymes, rhythms, and the like.
4. Notice when a child makes interesting shapes or patterns with small blocks, large blocks, pounding board shapes, playdough, or drawing materials. Notice if a child attempts to copy a pattern or if the pattern created is symmetrical. Notice also elaborate or unusual artwork in any media. Notice the process children go through as they plan their work.
5. Notice when a child appears to modify his or her language for less mature children. For example, a child might appropriately shorten sentences, use less sophisticated words, and change his or her pitch when speaking to very young children.
6. Notice when a child displays skill in putting together new or difficult puzzles, particularly if she or he examines the shape of puzzle pieces and seems to know where to place them without trial and error.
7. Notice when a child says or does something that indicates a sense of humor. For example, a child might pretend that the characteristics of one thing belong to another, as in a dog meowing.
8. Notice when a child expresses an understanding of abstract or complex concepts such as death, time, or electricity.
9. Notice when a child masters a new skill, a new concept, song, or rhyme with

unusual speed or when a child demonstrates a competence that has been presented in a lesson some time previously. For example, a child might independently use construction paper to assemble a witch, copying a technique demonstrated by a teacher some weeks earlier.

10. Notice when a child seems capable of locating him or herself in the environment. For example, does the child seem to know where everything is in the room and in the school building? When on a walk, can he or she tell how to get back to the school? Does the child maneuver his or her tricycle skillfully around the yard and seem to know when a space is too small to drive through? Does she or he understand how to keep out of the way of the swing?

11. Notice when children use language for a real exchange of ideas and information among themselves.

12. Notice when a child becomes totally absorbed in one kind of knowledge. For example, a boy or girl might spend all of his or her free time with cars and trucks, draw only cars and trucks, want to read books about cars and trucks, and talk knowledgeably about different types of cars and trucks.

13. Notice when a child displays great interest or skill in ordering and grouping items. For example, a child might create block constructions that are systematically organized by shape, sort toy vehicles by size and type, or spontaneously arrange pegboard pieces to form a rainbow-ordered color series.

14. Notice when a child takes apart and reassembles things with unusual skill.

15. Notice if a child identifies left or right, both in relation to his or her own body and the body of another person, or if she or he understands how to move to the left or right.

16. Notice when a child remembers and makes mental connections between past and present experiences. For instance, a child might spontaneously apply a principle learned in a group time about mammals to another lesson, weeks later, concerned with dinosaurs.

17. Notice when a child behaves in a way that indicates sensitivity to the needs or feelings of another child or adult. For example, a girl or boy might spontaneously help another child who had fallen or might move out of the way of another child without being asked.

18. Notice when a child is able to carry out complex instructions to do several things in succession or when a boy or girl is able to absorb several new concepts in a single session.

19. Notice when a child is unusually attentive to features of the classroom environment. For instance, a youngster might frequently be the first to notice a small change in the arrangement of the room, a teacher's new hairstyle, or a different picture on the wall.

20. Notice when a child uses verbal skills to handle conflict or to influence other children's behavior. For example, a child might use verbal skills to initiate

a toy exchange, to decide peer group activities, or to exercise general leadership (Roedell & Robinson, 1977).

Creating a Learning Atmosphere

Careful observation will help to identify specific strengths and weaknesses of individual children and show how much they vary in the maturity of their understanding in particular areas, the speed with which they can learn new concepts or skills, and their ability to organize information and generalize from one experience to another. Yet, while individual differences in children's abilities may have a dramatic influence on the content of a program, the basic principles that govern the learning and development of children of average intelligence apply equally well to the learning of gifted children.

The following four principles represent a synthesis of the work of many developmental psychologists, including Piaget (e.g., 1971), Bruner (e.g., Bruner, Olver, & Greenfield, 1966), Weikart (e.g., Weikart, et al., 1970), Baer (e.g., Risley & Baer, 1973), and Bandura (e.g., 1969). A more extensive discussion of psychological principles and their application to the learning of young children can be found in *Cognitive Development in Young Children* (Jackson, Robinson, & Dale, 1977), and *Social Development in Young Children* (Roedell, Slaby, & Robinson, 1977).

1. Children have a natural desire to learn that is maximized when new experiences are optimally matched with an individual child's previous experiences and existing level of understanding. Attention, comprehension, and memory are enhanced when each experience builds upon and expands previous experiences. The level of the optimal match may, of course, be different for gifted children.
2. Although young children can and do learn by quietly watching and listening, many ideas and skills are best learned when children have opportunities for active involvement—for touching, talking, and testing things on their own. Active involvement in learning may take place on an abstract or verbal level, as when children are given opportunities to predict what might happen in a given situation or to synthesize or evaluate what a teacher has said. Nonetheless, concrete materials may often be necessary to provide optimum opportunities for involving young children in the learning process, even when the concepts involved are advanced.
3. A child's tendency to perform or repeat particular behaviors is affected by the intrinsic interest of the activities, the extrinsic consequences produced by the behavior, and the behavioral models provided by teachers and other adults and children. In general, children will tend to repeat behaviors that attract the attention of people they know and like.

4. Children learn from each other. They learn skills by observing each other, and they communicate information to one another. In addition, the egalitarian nature of peer interaction provides a unique forum for the development of cognitive and motor, as well as social, skills. Communication skills are improved when children have ample opportunity to practice exchanging information with a variety of companions. Interaction with peers who have similar interests and abilities is as important for gifted children as it is for all children. Such peers, however, may be hard to locate. It should not be assumed that all children of similar chronological age will form a real peer group. Egalitarian interaction may not take place among children with widely differing abilities and interests.

Developing Social Skills

Social skills training is an essential part of every good preschool program (Combs & Slaby, 1978; Roedell, Slaby, & Robinson, 1977). Such training may be particularly important for gifted children who may find themselves in peer groups where they do not easily fit. A three-year-old who thinks like a six-year-old but has only average physical and social skills may have difficulty making friends. Communication with same-age peers may be quite difficult, particularly if a gifted child has acquired a vocabulary beyond the understanding of average three-year-olds. It may be equally difficult for gifted young children to overcome the physical and social differences between themselves and older children who are their peers in intellectual ability. Young children who are noticeably different may develop maladaptive patterns of social behavior that can make forming friendships even more difficult.

In focusing on social interaction skills, however, it should not be overlooked that gifted children also need to learn how to become independent learners. Children who are able to assume an independent role in creating their own learning challenges are more likely to make the most of their particular talents.

The development of both good social interaction and independent learning skills in gifted children is influenced by the same factors that govern the development of these skills in all young children. A well-planned physical environment, for example, can eliminate the need for constant direction from teachers by stimulating children to initiate and carry out their own activities. Child-size furniture, easily accessible, attractive materials, and an ordered physical setting can help children manage their own needs and clean up their own work areas. Materials that stimulate social interaction can be arranged to encourage small groups of children to develop activities together. For example, dress-up materials suggesting common themes, such as fire hats or medical equipment, can stimulate group fantasy play. "Gas station" requires at least two players; some swings and rocking equipment also require two or more cooperating children for successful operation.

Positive social behavior is facilitated by scheduling a smooth flow of interesting events. When materials are prepared in advance, children need not wait and run the risk of becoming bored. Providing sufficiently interesting and challenging activities can help direct children's natural energies toward problem-solving rather than toward disrupting the class. Like all children, gifted preschoolers may become either unruly or withdrawn when bored. However, the activities required to maintain their interest may need to be more complex than those required to maintain the interest of average children.

Teachers' behavior has a strong influence on children's social behavior. When adult attention focuses repeatedly on a particular child's behavior, that behavior is likely to increase; behavior that receives no attention tends to decrease in frequency. Children with advanced reasoning skills may be particularly adept at learning what reactions or responses their behavior will elicit. They can become experts at manipulating teacher attention. Teacher attention may be broadly defined to include conversation, smiling and watching a child, physical touching, or bringing special materials to enhance an activity. It may also include negative behaviors such as scolding or ridicule. Teachers, therefore, should be careful to concentrate their attention on children's appropriate behaviors, and ignore inappropriate behavior whenever possible. Misbehavior that cannot be ignored may be stopped in a matter-of-fact manner, with little comment. By focusing on children's strengths and successes, teachers help each child to develop positive feelings of self-esteem and self-confidence.

Directive statements from teachers should be kept to a minimum to allow children to form the habit of providing the initiative for their own behavior. Necessary directions can be imbedded in contingency statements that let the child know what must be accomplished before other events can take place. For example, a teacher might say, "As soon as you put away your paints, you'll be ready for a snack." In this way, the initiative for carrying out the behavior remains with the child. Negative contingency statements are also effective ways of informing children of the consequences of their negative behavior, for example, "If you throw sand again, you'll have to leave the sandbox" (Roedell, Slaby, & Robinson, 1977).

Peer conflicts can be minimized if teachers intervene and guide children to a peaceful resolution. At the Child Development Preschool, we have found that intellectually advanced preschoolers respond well to a problem-solving approach to conflict resolution. Often they have advanced verbal skills that enable them to communicate their needs successfully if given guidance by the teacher. The children's advanced reasoning skills help them generate many problem solutions. Teachers can encourage children to use these cognitive skills in everyday situations. Once a teacher defines a conflict as a problem in need of solution, children can use their logical skills to solve the problem (Hall & Roedell, 1978).

Planned teacher-directed lessons can also be successful ways of teaching appropriate social behavior to small groups of children. Using stories and puppets, teachers can guide children to think of alternative solutions to potential conflicts (Spivack & Shure, 1974). Puppets and role-modeling sessions can help children evaluate their solutions and learn to select alternatives that will bring about consequences they desire. Discussions of how children may run into conflicts in different situations can increase social sensitivity and awareness of the consequences of different social actions (Hall & Roedell, 1978; Roedell, Slaby, & Robinson, 1977). When aggressive conflicts do occur, teachers can step between the children and help the victim respond to the aggressor in an assertive way. Problem-solving guidance directed toward the aggressor should be saved for a neutral time. This procedure avoids reinforcing aggressive behavior with teacher attention (Roedell, Slaby, & Robinson, 1977).

Developing Thinking Skills

All good programs for preschool children focus to some extent on the development of thinking skills. Educators who follow a Piagetian model of education, for example, seek to help children develop such skills as classification, seriation, spatial relations, and temporal relations (Kamii & Radin, 1967; Weikart, Rogers, & Adcock, 1971). Many preschool programs focus on the development of language skills or on cognitive development in general (Gordon, 1972). In developing programs for gifted children, educators frequently use a model of intellectual development as a framework for building a curriculum to challenge these children's advanced thinking skills or develop their creative ability. The models offer teachers useful insights as well.

Benjamin Bloom, for example, has conceptualized the educational process in terms of rising hierarchical levels of thinking (Bloom, 1969). The six major levels illustrated in Table 4-1 are presented in the form of discrete activities, although in actual practice several levels of thinking might be combined in a single lesson. This model provides a useful conceptualization to guide teachers in planning learning experiences that encompass all levels of the hierarchy. Certainly gifted children, and average children too, should be provided with opportunities to go beyond mere memorization—to use facts to derive general principles, to generalize to other areas of interest, and to evaluate the appropriateness of their efforts. Sandra Kaplan (1975) has pointed out that bright children may pass through the lower levels of thinking more quickly than average children, giving more time to the development of higher levels. Gifted children, for example, are often quick to absorb basic facts. Nevertheless, the basics must be provided before children can advance to the higher levels. For instance,

Table 4-1
Bloom's Taxonomy of the Cognitive Domain
Illustrated with Sample Curriculum Activities

Taxonomy Level	Sample Activity
1. Knowledge	1. Children discuss information presented through books and pictures about the elements of a house and their functions.
2. Comprehension	2. Children sort items on a flannel board into things that belong to a house and things that do not.
3. Application	3. Children arrange pre-cut elements of a house on a flannel board. They create a story about building a house and illustrate it using the flannel pieces.
4. Analysis	4. Children make a poster analyzing a house into its parts. They show the outside walls, doors, and windows on the outside of a folded piece of paper and the different furniture that belongs to rooms on the inside of the fold. Inside, rooms are organized according to function (e.g., kitchen, bedroom, living room, etc.)
5. Synthesis	5. Children design and build models of their own ideal houses. They make clay models using pieces of cloth, sawdust, popsicle sticks, and so on, as props.
6. Evaluation	6. Children decide which houses would work best in different climates and tell why. For instance, a house with open walls might work best in a warm climate; a house with a sloping roof might work best in a rainy climate, and so on. (This stage might be combined with synthesis, so that children incorporate the needs of different climates into their house designs.)

children will be limited in the extent to which they benefit from a learning center filled with a variety of measuring tools if they are never shown the basic rules and principles of how such tools are used (Bailey & Leonard, 1977).

Guilford (1967), in his model of the Structure of Intellect, conceptualizes intelligence in the form of a cube. Its three dimensions indicate the three components of a given intellectual act: its operation, its content, and its product. Content refers to different types of subject matter. Operation refers to the process or processes by which the intellect engages the different forms of content. The final dimension, the product, refers to the outcome when an operation works on content. The model and its implications for curriculum development are explained in detail by Mary Meeker in her book *The Structure of Intellect: Its Interpretation and Uses* (1969).

The Guilford model is particularly useful for teachers who wish to help children develop independent, creative thinking skills. Guilford points to the importance of activities designed to enhance divergent thinking skills and to encourage students to think of many alternative solutions to a problem. Traditional education too often focuses on convergent thinking, encouraging students to find a single correct solution to a problem. By conceptualizing intellectual activities as combinations of operations, contents, and products, teachers can vary different aspects of the curriculum to meet different goals. For example, different kinds of thinking processes—cognition, memory, convergent production, divergent production, and evaluation—can all be applied to similar content, yielding different products. Or a particular type of thinking skill, such as divergent production, can be applied to different types of content.

Frank Williams (1970) has also suggested that curriculum development be considered in terms of three dimensions—but here the three are the subject matter content, the teacher's strategies of teaching, and the student's cognitive and affective responses to the learning situation. Williams is concerned with encouraging teachers to help children develop skills in creative problem-solving and original expression. He includes affective responses in his model to help teachers realize the importance to learning of such noncognitive factors as risk-taking, curiosity, and imagination. The Williams model is explained in detail, together with curriculum ideas tied to each objective, in his book *Classroom Ideas for Encouraging Thinking and Feeling* (1970).

The main advantage to teachers of using these curriculum models is the perspective they provide on the process of education. To be effective, teachers need to define their task as something more than just imparting information to children. Teaching involves helping children exercise a broad range of thinking skills while developing appropriate attitudes about learning. Only by including objectives for both cognitive and affective skills in their curricula can teachers be consistent in their attempts to develop the full range of children's abilities (Sisk, 1977).

Acceleration vs. Enrichment

Psychologists and educators agree that one of the keys to good teaching lies in finding the optimum match mentioned earlier between the student's level of understanding and the material presented for learning. The most effective learning takes place when children are provided with experiences that slightly stretch their level of sophistication. Children are less likely to devote their attention either to material that is completely familiar and well understood or to material that is so advanced as to be incomprehensible (Furth, 1970; Hunt, 1961; Piaget, 1966). The most important issue to be solved in educating gifted children is how this optimum match of learning material with competence level is to be provided.

Many educators believe that gifted children should be provided with additional materials at the same level they have reached in a particular subject area, rather than being allowed to progress to the next highest level. The emphasis is on "enrichment" rather than "acceleration." The distinction between enrichment and acceleration may disappear when actual educational activities are discussed. For example, many preschool curricula include opportunities for children to engage in sink-and-float experiments. An enriched sink-and-float experiment for gifted children might include having the children make charts to record which of their experimental objects sank and which floated. This type of enrichment is, of course, also a form of acceleration since children engaging in this form of experiment are performing activities usually performed by older children in elementary school.

The enrichment-acceleration argument comes into focus when subject areas such as reading are discussed. A child who has learned all the letters and letter sounds and is constantly asking teachers to identify and spell words is probably ready to learn to read. No amount of enrichment activities involving new and different ways to study individual letters will satisfy this child's curiosity about the written word. Likewise, it makes little sense to ignore such a child's enthusiasm for reading and try to fill his or her time with enrichment unrelated to the skill in question. In such cases, the only way to provide the optimal match between children's level of competence and learning material is to provide the appropriate material and allow children to proceed with the skills-learning they are ready to accomplish.

When considered in this light, it becomes clear that the word acceleration is an unfortunate label for activities such as teaching reading to preschoolers who are ready to learn. In a classroom where gifted children are not allowed to move ahead according to their own rapid developmental rate, their progress has been decelerated. When an educational program does keep pace with a child's rapid learning rate, the result is not really acceleration; the child is not being pushed ahead at an unnatural rate. A better description of the process is to say that the classroom environment is adapting to a child's need for rapid progress. The issues involved in the acceleration-enrichment debate are discussed in detail in Lynn Fox's (1979) chapter in the 78th *NSSE Yearbook,* "Programs for the Gifted and Talented: An Overview." As she states:

If "enrichment" is defined as the provision of learning experiences that develop higher processes of thinking and creativity in a subject area, and if "acceleration" is defined as the adjustment of learning time to meet the individual capabilities of the students, the two terms are complementary rather than conflicting. If one assumes that the goal of educational programs for the gifted is to meet their learning needs, *both* enrichment and acceleration are necessary. Thus, the gifted learner can proceed at a faster pace, to a higher level of content, and to more abstract and evaluative thinking than his age-peers. (pp. 106–107)

EVALUATION OF PROGRAMS FOR GIFTED YOUNG CHILDREN

Generally the evidence from a broad range of studies concerned with children from diverse backgrounds indicates that preschool attendance tends to benefit all children (e.g., Gordon, 1972). However, efforts to evaluate the effects of programs designed specifically for gifted preschool children have only just begun. The evaluator of such programs faces two major problems. The first problem lies in the difficulty of showing a positive change for children whose pretest scores are already far above the mean of the rest of the population. IQ gains, for example, can hardly be expected from a group of children whose mean IQ is already at the 99th percentile. Evaluation of academic achievement poses the same problem, with the added difficulty that academic achievement tests normed for preschool-aged children do not allow them to demonstrate the advanced academic skills of which they are often capable. The second problem is a more philosophical one. When children score below average levels on tests of intelligence or of academic skill, the obvious goal of a program is to raise their scores toward the mean of the general population. When children score far above the mean, however, the program goal is less clear. How much improvement in areas such as academic skill should be expected of children who are already advanced?

The staff of the Child Development Preschool has adopted the following approaches to these evaluation problems. IQ gains for children in the program have not been expected. Academic achievement has been assessed with the Peabody Individual Achievement Test (see Chapter 3 for a description). In the absence of age-appropriate percentile norms, children's performance has been evaluated using raw scores with reference to age and grade equivalents to provide a context for interpretation. In addition, the age equivalent of each child's test score was compared with the child's chronological age at time of testing. Fall and spring testing during the 1976–77 and 1977–78 academic years showed that children maintained their mean degree of advancement in academic skills during both years, in addition to making significant raw score gains on each PIAT subtest.

Looking at the preschool group as a whole, however, obscures the vast individual differences that exist in the children's academic motivation and skill. The program goals of the Child Development Preschool have been individualized to allow each child to progress at his or her own rate academically. The result has been that some children have made tremendous academic progress, while others have showed more modest gains. For example, one boy started the program in the fall of 1976 at the age of four years, six months, with a total PIAT grade equivalent score of 2.6. By the spring of 1978, when he was only six years old, he was scoring at a grade equivalent of 5.1. His most rapid acceleration was in the area of mathematics. His mathematics grade equivalent score rose from 1.9 in fall 1976 to 7.0 in spring 1978. Other students made more modest gains, moving from the kindergarten level to the first grade level during the course of a year.

A program can also be evaluated in terms of development of skills other than those for which the children were selected. For example, one goal of the Child Development Preschool has been to increase the children's repertoire of social skills, both in interacting with peers and in directing their own learning. Although children have not been selected for advanced social development, the school's philosophy is that they will be better able to make use of their intellectual and academic gifts if they are well adjusted socially. Direct observation of social interactions and teacher ratings of social-emotional characteristics have been used to evaluate this aspect of the program. Results suggest that children increased their cooperative social interactions and their ability to overcome obstacles and to talk with peers and decreased their nagging, negative behaviors during the course of the year (Child Development Research Group, 1978; Roedell, 1978).

In addition to direct measures of skill development, evaluators often turn to indirect measures of program success. Parent satisfaction is one such measure. Measures of parent satisfaction include questionnaires, the number of children who re-enroll, and numbers of program applicants. Another indirect source of information in program effectiveness is follow-up data on program graduates. Children whose advanced intellectual and academic talents are documented at an early age may be more likely to be placed in appropriate programs early in their school careers (Robinson, Roedell, & Jackson, 1979).

All these measures provide some information about program effects. Given the paucity of information on the performance of gifted preschool children who do not attend special programs, however, the information derived from these measures is difficult to interpret. A major problem is the lack of a research data base against which program goals can be realistically established and evaluated. The state of the art regarding gifted children invites comparison with past efforts undertaken in behalf of disadvantaged children. Although in many important ways evaluation research with preschool programs for gifted children does differ from research with compensatory programs, there is a strong similarity to the status of research that existed in the mid-1960s. At that time there were a number of basic needs that required resolution. There was need, first of all, for program development, that is, for the development and debugging of discrete, articulated models designed for the target population. Second, specific, appropriate measures had to be developed that were consonant with the goals of the program and the ability levels of the children. Finally—and this last step took longest to recognize—payoff of the programs had to be measured in long-range, not short-range, terms. It is only now, for example, that behavioral scientists and educational specialists (e.g., Lazar et al., 1977; Research Report, 1977) are developing a body of data showing that the effects of high-quality compensatory early childhood programs do not "wash out" but indeed can be detected many years later using school achievement and school placement criteria.

Analogous work with preschool programs for gifted children has not yet even begun. Goals for such programs are not clear; program models are not fully articulated; outcome measures do not exist; and no appropriate time span has been envisioned. There are no compairson data to indicate what happens to the performance of gifted young children who do not participate in preschool programs of any kind or who enroll in ordinary preschools. There is good reason to believe that the basic questions surrounding the development of effective educational programs for gifted young children can only be answered through carefully planned, long-term research efforts. It seems probable that differences between gifted preschool children who participate in a special program and those who do not may not be evident until later on in their school careers.

DESCRIPTIONS OF SAMPLE PROGRAMS

There are many approaches to educating gifted preschool children, and many interesting and worthwhile programs are currently in operation across the nation. No single volume could attempt to describe them all. Consideration of programs, therefore, will be limited to a few representative samples of the main approaches to educating young gifted children—those that are traditional, those that stress creativity, and those designed for the handicapped. In addition, a program using parents as teachers will be discussed as well as The Seattle Child Development Preschool. Not all the programs are limited to the gifted only. The information presented has been obtained, in most instances, from the program operators themselves. In many cases the available data were limited to a rather general description of program goals.

One of the best ways to get a real feel for a particular program is to visit and observe teachers and students interacting with one another. Readers who are interested in a detailed, practical understanding of the operation of any program for gifted children are encouraged to visit, observe, and talk with the teachers.

Traditional Programs

Many programs for gifted preschool-aged children are part of a larger school that serves children through the elementary school years and in some cases through high school. The continuity of educational programming offered by such institutions provides a major advantage for children who remain enrolled throughout their school years. Such programs frequently tend to focus on the teaching of traditional academic skills along with the social skills essential for optimum classroom functioning.

The *Hunter College Elementary School*, a public school program on the Hunter College campus in New York City, is one of the oldest of the traditional programs for gifted children. Children are accepted into the preschool division of the program at age three years, six months. Screening includes administration of the Stanford-Binet IQ test. Information is sought from the tester concerning the child's behavior during the test session. Detailed information is also obtained from the parents. Children from disadvantaged backgrounds may be identified for entrance on the basis of leadership and creative potential. Although the nursery school fosters an air of playful productivity, traditional academic skills are taught together with a second language—Spanish—and children are involved in special independent projects (Mancini, 1977; Miller, 1978).

The *Astor Program* is another public school program in New York City. Level I of the Astor Program serves four-and-a-half- to five-and-a-half-year-old chidren who score in the 98th percentile (IQ 132 or above) on the Stanford-Binet; who demonstrate social maturity in an interview situation; and who are observed, in their home or current school, to have long attention spans, an ability to delay impulsivity, and good skills in following directions. The Astor Program emphasizes the higher level thinking skills outlined in Bloom's taxonomy, logic, and the ability to evaluate the social consequences of different courses of action. Children are also taught basic academic skills, with advanced work as individuals become ready. Teachers stimulate creative investigation of different content areas of interest to students and encourage children to formulate questions, form hypotheses, and test and evaluate their speculations (Ehrlich, in press; Kaplan, 1978).

The *Roeper School,* a private school for gifted children in Bloomfield Hills, Michigan, serves children ages three to twelve in the lower school component of its program. Children are taught in multi-age groupings in an open concept environment. Affective education is stressed, along with learning through small group interchanges and creative approaches to problem-solving through the use of divergent thinking skills (Roeper, 1966; 1978).

In Seattle, Washington, there are two private schools that serve gifted children from preschool age through elementary school. In describing the program of *Seattle Country Day School,* its director echoes the philosophy of many of the traditional programs: "We want to get on with the business of learning for kids who are ready" (Beckman, 1978). Applicants to Seattle Country Day are tested with the WPPSI or WISC-R, parents and children are interviewed, and information from previous schools is accumulated when available. Children must show social maturity as well as academic talent before being admitted. The program emphasizes building a good foundation of academic skills. The *Evergreen School,* which serves children from preschool through junior high school, seeks three- and four-year-old children who show evidence of creativity as well as intellectual advancement. Three-year-olds are selected by teacher observation of their behavior during a visit to the classroom during the spring. Such children usually qualify on the basis of IQ by age four, when applicants are tested. The program stresses group cooperation, preacademic skills, and independence in work and play (Christensen, 1978).

Programs That Stress Creativity

The *Creative Learning Center* in Dallas, Texas, has a program for 60 gifted children between the ages of two and eight. Two-thirds of the children come from poverty backgrounds; 50 percent are black, 25 percent Chicano, 15 percent American Indian, and 10 percent Anglo. Screening includes a home visit, a parent and child interview, and testing by a psychologist. While the focus of the program is on creativity, a wide range of academic areas is covered. Both Spanish and English are spoken at the Center. The program has been influenced by the Montessori method. Children proceed at their own pace using self-correcting, easily accessible materials in a programmed learning environment. The teacher serves as an observer and facilitator and encourages each child to develop a sense of independence (Tittle, 1978).

A Small World—A Center for Creativity in Boise, Idaho, emphasizes developing the creativity inherent in every child. The program director reports that, although there is no formal selection procedure beyond parent nomination, many of the children in the program demonstrate advanced skills such as early reading (Comba, 1978). The philosophy of the school is based on the assumption that every child is gifted in some area and that the task of the school is to discover and develop each child's gifts as well as his or her potential in all other areas. Individual programs are planned by teachers to match individual children's abilities and interests.

Programs for Gifted and Talented Handicapped Children

The *Sunburst Preschool,* sponsored by the Panhandle Child Development Association in Coeur d'Alene and Post Falls, Idaho, serves handicapped children and nonhandicapped children from rural backgrounds, who score above the mean on the Peabody Picture Vocabulary Test, the Columbia Mental Maturity Scale, or the Draw-A-Person test. The program has been designated as a model program and has been funded by the U.S. Office of Education, Office of Gifted and Talented. The program's goals are to provide individually planned learning experiences that fit the strengths and weaknesses of each child; to keep every child "turned on" to learning; and to challenge the development of higher level thinking processes through development of concepts. The curriculum is based on Bloom's taxonomy of thinking skills, with lessons planned to guide children from the lower levels of knowledge and comprehension through the higher levels of synthesis and evaluation. Each group of lessons is planned around a theme that engages the children in increasingly complex thought processes.

If individualization of programming is important for gifted and talented preschoolers in general, it is essential for those who have some sort of handicap. The Sunburst Preschool program highlights this necessity for individualization. Parent volunteers assist teachers in the classroom, working on a one-to-one basis with children. Each child's program is planned, and each child's progress is assessed via reference to specific criterion listed in a concept-assessment strategy. Basic concepts intended to facilitate transition into a public school setting are part of each plan, as is a set of diagnostic activities to help determine where the child is and how far he or she has to progress. Assessment dates are recorded on the plan, along with dates when the teaching of concepts was begun. Beside each concept is a space for recording the highest level of thinking, as defined by Bloom's taxonomy, reached by a child in relation to each concept. A copy of the assessment sheet is given to the child's public school teacher upon first grade entrance or advanced school placement. A sample section of the assessment package can be found in Table 4-2. Children are also administered the Peabody Individual Achievement Test for evaluation of specific academic skills (Hanninen, 1978).

The *Gifted-Handicapped Preschool Project* in Chapel Hill, North Carolina, provides another model for serving preschool children, ages three to six, who show unusual gifts or talents in spite of physical, mental, emotional, or experiential handicaps. The program is financed by the U.S. Office of Education, Bureau of the Handicapped. Children are referred to the project by parents, physicians, teachers, or other professionals. A child's outstanding performance area may be in general intellectual ability, in a particular academic aptitude, in creative or productive thinking, in leadership ability, in psychomotor ability, or in the visual or performing arts. A handicapped child who is at least one year above the norm for his or her age in any of these areas is eligible for the program.

Teachers are encouraged to use a combination of four techniques to identify potential participants for the program: (1) unstructured observation of the child's behavior in the classroom, noting particular skills; (2) checklists to obtain specific information about a child's capabilities in particular areas; (3) structured observations in which a specific child's behaviors are counted for specified time periods; and (4) sociometric measures with which teachers ask children for their opinions of which of their classmates would perform well in different situations.

The program's curriculum is structured to provide each child with a broad range of experiences through a unit-concept approach. Instruction is organized around a central theme and encompasses different activities designed to stretch the child's thinking capabilities to the higher levels outlined in Bloom's taxonomy. The Chapel Hill curriculum considers the taxonomy to be a continuum of skills, rather than six discrete levels of functioning.

Children in the program participate in recreation, music, art, play, and individual therapy as needed. In all areas of instruction, the program is built

Table 4-2

Sample Sheet from a Criterion-Referenced Concept Assessment
Developed by the Sunburst Preschool

Thinking Process	Area	Concept	Activities	Dates			
				Assessed	Start Teaching	Completed	Retested
	Expressive Language	Identifying	1. Verbalizes understanding of seasons 2. Can verbalize differences, e.g., what is the difference between wood, glass? 3. Verbalizes causal relationships, e.g., tell me what would happen if... 4. Can rhyme words.				
	Expressive Language	Identifying	1. Can describe likes and dislikes (and give reasons why). 2. Can give synonyms for simple words; pretty, good, yummy, big, little, hard, scary, fun, fast, slow.				

around the handicapped children's abilities, rather than their disabilities. Individual objectives are devised for each child, providing a balance of activities to challenge the child's strengths as well as to help remediate his or her handicap.

Parent involvement is a critical aspect of the program. Parents assist teachers in the classroom and are encouraged to carry on program activities at home with their child (Blacher-Dixon, 1977; Child Development Institute, 1977).

The *RAPYHT Program* (Retrieval and Acceleration of Promising Young Handicapped and Talented) is located at the Institute for Child Behavior and Development at the University of Illinois, Champaign-Urbana, Illinois. The program is sponsored by the U.S. Office of Education, Bureau of the Handicapped. Preschool-aged children are identified for the program at the time of screening for special education. Since the talents of handicapped children may be obscured by the handicap during initial screening, special education teachers are asked to complete talent checklists for students enrolled in their classrooms to identify those whose special gifts were missed in the preliminary screen.

The RAPYHT Program incorporates two distinct approaches for educating gifted handicapped preschoolers—the open classroom and the structured classroom. In both kinds of classrooms, the gifted handicapped are integrated with children who have no handicap and with nontalented handicapped children to provide a mainstream setting and to demonstrate the suitability of the classroom approaches for a wide range of children.

In the open classroom, the teacher helps children acquire basic skills and provides an environment that encourages and nurtures specific talents while meeting the children's special needs. The philosophy of the program is based upon the assumption that children are the best judges of what, when, how, and at what pace they should learn. Children initiate their own learning activities; teachers serve as facilitators. Teachers base curriculum on the children's interests and attempt to extend children's learning in activities of their choice. A broad range of materials are readily available to the children at all times. Problems are discussed and resolved by teachers and children working together. By providing encouragement, feedback, guidance, information, and clarification, teachers create a purposeful atmosphere in the classroom. Children are expected to use time productively and to value work and learning. The classroom schedule is flexible, and children may work independently or in small groups. During the daily group meeting, all children and teachers meet together to plan the day's activities.

In contrast to the open classroom approach, the RAPYHT Program includes a structured, teacher-directed classroom with a curriculum based on Guilford's Structure of Intellect (SOI) model. The philosophy of this approach rests on the assumption that children learn best through sequenced activities presented by teachers, each of which has specific and individualized instructional objectives. The SOI model serves as a basis for planned programming to foster a variety of intellectual abilities, including convergent, divergent, and evaluative thinking. Math, language, and prereading lessons are presented in a game format. Music, art, dance, and activities designed to enhance social-emotional development are included. Activities are planned for individuals or for small groups of children with similar needs. Short periods of structured lessons alternate with directed play time, during which children initiate their own projects.

Classroom assessment procedures are incorporated into both teaching approaches to determine each child's developmental level in all areas. Individualized Education Programs (IEPs) are prepared for each child in areas of strength as well as in areas of deficit. Children's progress is charted periodically by teachers (Karnes & Bertschi, 1978). Preliminary evaluation indicates that children in both classrooms of the RAPYHT Program have made gains in IQ and on tests of visual-motor and verbal skills (Karnes, 1977).

A Program Using Parents as Teachers

Project L-E-A-P (Learning and Enrichment for Able Preschoolers) at Dundalk Community College, Baltimore, Maryland, served children between the ages of four and six. The program is no longer in operation due to lack of funding, but the model is an interesting one. Children were identified using Piagetian tests of classification, one-to-one correspondence, conservation of mass, and seriation, as well as the Peabody Picture Vocabulary Test. Children who performed sufficiently well on the Piagetian tasks and who obtained an IQ of 120 or above were admitted to the program. The children, their parents, and the project director met Saturday mornings for three hours, during which time the parents worked with their own children under the guidance of the director. Parents were responsible for recording their child's reactions to and use of materials according to a prescribed format. The curriculum emphasized fast-paced, individualized instruction in prereading and reading skills, arithmetical concepts, and general language arts development. In each subject area, individual children's skills were evaluated, and learning experiences individually appropriate to each child's level of advancement were provided (Schuster, 1976).

The Seattle Project

The *Child Development Preschool* at the University of Washington in Seattle, Washington, has been funded as a model program by the U.S. Office of Education, Office of the Gifted and Talented. Funding for some aspects of the program has also been supplied by the Spencer Foundation. The preschool is an integral part of the Child Development Research Group's comprehensive program of research and service, which focuses on the development of children with different types of advanced intellectual and academic skills.

The preschool program is the first link in a series of educational programs for intellectually and academically advanced children in Seattle. The Individual Progress Program, a Seattle public school program for extraordinarily able elementary students, is designed to allow students to move through an enriched academic curriculum at their own pace. The Early Entrance Program, sponsored by the Child Development Research Group at the University of Washington, provides extraordinarily advanced junior high school students with the opportunity to enroll part- or full-time at the University of Washington.

The screening system developed by the Seattle project is described in Chapter 3. Some children qualify for the program by demonstrating generally advanced intellectual abilities; others qualify on the basis of advanced abilities in specific cognitive areas. Information is obtained from parent questionnaires and from testing the children.

The program is designed to offer a variety of learning experiences in a balanced mixture of teacher- and child-structured situations. Children are placed in small groups according to their competence levels to work with teachers on structured activities in language arts, reading, science, mathematics, social skills learning, art, drama, and creative movement. Physical skills are developed through planned activities involving large and small muscles. An attempt is made to match instructional activities with each child's level of competence in each area.

The Child Development Preschool recognizes the fact that preschool children are ready and eager to learn academic concepts not usually taught until an older age. Academic tasks designed for older children, however, are often not appealing to young children because they tend to require the children to carry out teacher-directed tasks while sitting still and concentrating on written worksheets or to read and follow written instructions. Many three- and four-year-old children, no matter how bright, quickly lose interest in activities presented in these ways. Advanced activities are adapted, therefore, to provide advanced content in a format more acceptable to young children. Lessons are broken into shorter units, location of work is varied within a lesson, visual demonstrations are given as often as possible, activities are presented as games, and attractive manipulative materials are provided so that children have something to hold on to and experiment with.

Many programs for gifted children accept only children who demonstrate social maturity. At the Child Development Preschool, however, the development of social skills is a critical element of the preschool curriculum rather than a criterion for admission. Five categories of social skills are emphasized:

1. Independence. Children learn to assume responsibility for self-help routines; they learn to direct their own activities, make decisions, and follow through with their plans; they learn to focus their attention and continue their activities even when others are near and likely to interfere.

2. Assertiveness. Children learn to stand up for their rights in nonviolent, assertive ways; they learn to express needs and emotions effectively without resorting to crying or whining.
3. Social sensitivity. Children learn to interpret and understand the needs and feelings of other people; they learn to help, share, and cooperate with others.
4. Making friendships. Children learn to interact with other children and with adults; they learn how to ask others to join group activities and to respond appropriately to overtures from other children; they learn to mesh their own interests with those of others while participating in group activities.
5. Solving problems. Children learn to negotiate differences and to solve conflicts without resorting to physical violence.

These skills are taught through teacher guidance throughout the day and through planned lessons involving stories, puppets, and role-playing.

Children's progress in the program is evaluated in several ways. Teachers keep ongoing behavioral records that are summarized in a final report listing each child's skills in each area of the curriculum. A sample section of a final evaluation report is given in Table 4–3. Children are also evaluated with a battery of standardized tests, including the Peabody Individual Achievement Test (Roedell & Robinson, 1977).

EARLY ENTRANCE TO SCHOOL

There are few areas in education that cause as much controversy as the prospect of some form of acceleration. Strangely enough, all available research evidence indicates that shortening the period of schooling for students who are intellectually advanced and socially mature is a beneficial practice (see, e.g., Daurio, 1977; Gallagher, 1975). One major advantage of educational acceleration is that it allows gifted students to enter their careers at an earlier age. As Lehman (1953) noted, gifted individuals in many fields tend to be most productive during their early years. Brilliant mathematicians, for example, tend to make their breakthrough discoveries at ages when most students have not yet been awarded their Ph.D. degrees (Stanley, 1977). Educational adjustments that shorten the extended educational periods of gifted children can be beneficial to both the individual and the culture (Gallagher, 1975).

For intellectually advanced preschool-aged children, early school entrance provides an excellent educational option. By entering school early, such children can be provided with an effective match of learning materials to readiness level, and, at the same time, experience a form of acceleration that is least disruptive to the continuity of education. It is probably far better for some children to enter school early and progress along with classmates than to enter school at a later age and experience boredom with an unchallenging curriculum

Table 4–3
Sample Section of a Final Evaluation from
the Child Development Preschool

Child's Name_____ Curriculum Area____Math_____

Skills child has demonstrated in this curriculum area
(Including social, physical, and cognitive skills as they relate to activities in this area):

Counts at least to 25 sequentially. Counts objects to 8 before beginning to lose track. Recognizes numerals to 20.

Creates beautifully symmetrical designs in block arrangements or drawings.

Extremely good spatial ability. Draws with perspective. (Can draw a three-dimensional staircase; draws objects smaller that are farther away.)

Good at map-reading, spatial orientation.

Can reproduce a complex pattern of 8 attribute blocks perfectly.

Cuisenaire rods: Can verbalize relationships among length of rods; builds staircases.

Does simple addition and subtraction accurately, using counters.

Geometric shapes: Can find different combinations of blocks to fill in a given pattern.

Sets, logic and attributes: Grasps concepts of set, empty set, subset. Can compare numbers of objects in sets accurately. Categorizes accurately by attributes. Grasps unspoken criteria for sets. Can identify which block is missing from a set and can name its attributes. Grasps and verbalizes a one-difference relationship.

Works well with a partner. Long attention to solving a problem. Accurate and neat.

Skills in this curriculum area which the child should work on developing next:

Continue work with:
  Writing numerals
  Keeping track when counting above 8
  Recording system for Cuisenaire rod problems; continue with rods
  Intersection of sets; more work with logic
  Tangrams (too difficult for him now)
  Graphs
  Measurements
  Geoblocks—more advanced spatial work.

or be skipped one or more grades during the course of education.

A number of studies have examined the results of early entrance to school —all with generally positive results. Hobson (1948) reported follow-up data on high school students who had been early school entrants in 1932. The early entrants exceeded their older classmates in grades earned and in academic honors. In addition, the early entrants participated in more extracurricular activities (although fewer contact sports) than regular students, and a larger percentage of early entrants went on to some type of post-secondary education. More recently,

Braga (1969; 1971) evaluated the progress of mentally advanced children who had been admitted to school early (early admit group), compared with a random sample of average children admitted at the regular time (normal admit group), and a group with IQs similar to the early entrants but approximately one year older (late admit group). The late admit group was representative of children who could have been early entrants, but whose parents chose to keep them with their chronological age peers. Results showed no significant differences between the early admit group and either of the other groups on achievement tests, school records, parent and teacher questionnaires, or teacher ratings of general behavior, motivation, and work habits in grades 1, 3 or 7. In the fifth grade, the early admit group was rated as more highly motivated than the late admit group. These findings are particularly interesting since the early admit children, seven months younger on the average than their classmates, were compared with older children who were equally bright and who, therefore, had higher mental ages. In spite of these positive findings, the teachers in the same schools that sponsored this early entrance program were, as a group, highly unfavorable to the practice of early admission. Their beliefs, which were completely at odds with the data many of them had helped to collect, were that early entrants lack social, emotional, and physical maturity, need more supervision, are unable to work independently, do not finish assignments, tire easily, are restless, and are frustrated by competition with older children. Many of these teachers had had early entrants in their classes and had thus provided the data documenting the success of the early entrants. The pupils admitted early had not, of course, been identified as early entrants to their teachers.

Other research efforts have confirmed the results of the Hobson and Braga studies (see, e.g., Birch et al., 1965; Daurio, 1977; Gallagher, 1975; Getzels & Dillon, 1973; Paschal, 1960; Reynolds, 1962; Terman & Oden, 1947). Since mental age generally has been found to be more highly correlated than chronological age with academic achievement (Birch et al., 1965), these findings are not surprising.

Of course these studies reflect the results of early admission to school based upon a complete evaluation of the child previous to acceptance into the program. Children whose development is uneven and whose advanced intellectual skills are not accompanied by equivalent social and physical maturity might not benefit from acceleration in their education at the time of school entrance. Such students might well benefit, however, from accelerative practices later on.

SUMMARY

Programs developed for gifted children must take into account the extreme diversity represented within this population. The program should provide individualized opportunities for development in cognitive, physical, and social skill areas and should include extra stimulation for skills targeted in the identification system.

Several different program models have been developed. There is no evidence to indicate which of the models is most effective. Actually there may be no "best" program model. In the comparisons of Head Start programs undertaken by David Weikart (Research Report, 1977), for example, it was found that all models were effective when teachers were committed to the model and dedicated to the children. This same principle may well hold true for programs designed to serve gifted children. The intense interaction of teachers and children involved in learning about topics of interest to both may be the formula for producing an effective program, no matter which model is followed.

Different program models have different goals for children. This diversity of goals is essential in a pluralistic society with multiple, and often conflicting, goals for children. Parents need a choice in determining the best educational program for their child. The program that is perfect for one child may well be the wrong choice for another.

5

CONCLUSION

THE CONTENT OF this monograph reflects our conviction that those who wish to learn about gifted young children must begin by considering what is known about young children in general, about the measurement of attributes such as intelligence and creativity, and about the characteristics of gifted children. This information helps define the issues that are likely to be important in planning for gifted young children and suggests identification tools and program models that show some promise of effectiveness.

On the other hand, generalizations about the specific needs of gifted young children or the relative merits of different assessment instruments or instructional programs cannot be made safely without first testing their applicability to particular groups of gifted young children. This is what we have done at the Seattle project and what others are doing across the nation. Program developers have had to struggle to define their objectives and to work out techniques for meeting those objectives without access to any coherent, research-based statements that specify the ways in which particular groups of gifted young children are likely to be similar to, or different from, other young children. Programs have been developed and implemented on the basis of assumptions that may be quite inappropriate.

One generalization in need of basic research concerns the question of program objectives. The criteria for evaluating preschool programs adopted by federal agencies, for example, were established in the context of the compensatory education movement. Because the children served by compensatory programs clearly lack some of the basic intellectual and academic readiness skills important for success in school, improvement in these skills has been the primary criterion for judging the short-term effectiveness of the programs. There is no reason why such criteria for programs for gifted preschool children could not eventually be adopted, despite the fact that some tricky methodological problems are involved (see Chapters 2 and 4). However, gifted young children are not particularly likely to be deficient in these skills. In fact, they may be remarkably proficient. Are intellectual and academic gains, then, always the most appropriate measure of program effectiveness?

To justify such an evaluation basis, we need first to document the fact that such gains will have some long-term beneficial effect on gifted children's school careers. This may be the case. It is equally possible, however, that the principal advantages of preschool programs for gifted young children will be found to rest in other types of outcomes.

One such outcome may be the documentation of the abilities of academically gifted young children before they begin their public school careers. Given the poor record of kindergarten teachers in identifying academically able children and the probable negative consequences if their abilities go unrecognized (Sutherland & Goldschmidt, 1974), better identification of such gifted children may by itself have a substantial positive impact on their school careers. Perhaps, though, identification alone is not enough. A potential benefit of all preschool programs for gifted children is the opportunity for their parents to get to know one another and share their experiences. What would be the impact of a program that functioned solely as a support group for parents of gifted young children? But again, identification and the establishment of parent support groups may have substantially less impact than a preschool program that provides gifted young children with opportunities to work and play together. One crucial outcome of such a program may be the opportunity it provides for academically able and otherwise gifted children to develop friendships with others who share their abilities and interests and to learn that they need not always be "different" just because they are unusually talented.

Finally, the long-term significance of a program for academically gifted young children might be a function of the extent to which the children develop a positive attitude toward both learning and school situations. If their first experience with education is a joyful one, perhaps they will be motivated to endure the boredom and frustrations that may be unavoidable later in the primary school years.

The answers to important questions such as these will be found only if skilled researchers and program developers collaborate on carefully designed and thorough studies of the characteristics of various groups of gifted young children and the long-term impact of different educational experiences on their educational achievement and personal adjustment. As more funds become available to serve gifted children, it is imperative, we believe, that some of these funds be devoted to supporting such research efforts.

REFERENCES

Abraham, W. Counseling the gifted. *Focus on Guidance*, 1976, *9*, 1–11.

Alpern, G.D., & Boll, T.J. *Developmental profile*. Indianapolis: Psychological Development Publication, 1972.

Bachelder, B.L., & Denny, M.R. A theory of intelligence: I. Span and the complexity of stimulus control. *Intelligence*, 1977, *1*, 127–150.

Bailey, D.B., & Leonard, J. A. Model for adapting Bloom's taxonomy to a preschool curriculum for the gifted. *The Gifted Child Quarterly*, 1977, *21*, 97–102.

Baltes, P. *Life span developmental psychology: Introduction to research methods*. Monterey, CA: Brooks/Cole, 1977.

Bandura, A. Social-learning theory of identification processes. In D.A. Goslin (Ed.), *Handbook of socialization theory and research*. Chicago: Rand McNally, 1969.

Barbe, W.B. Characteristics of gifted children. *Educational Administration and Supervision*, 1955, *41*, 207–217.

Barbe, W.B. A study of the family background of the gifted. *Journal of Educational Psychology*, 1956, *47*, 302–309.

Bayley, N. Consistency and variability in the growth of intelligence from birth to eighteen years. *The Journal of Genetic Psychology*, 1949, *75*, 165–196.

Beckman, L. Personal communication, April 1978.

Birch, J.W., Tisdall, W.J., Barney, W.D., & Marks, C.N. *A field demonstration of the effectiveness and feasibility of early admission to school for mentally advanced children* (Cooperative Research Project D-010). Pittsburgh: University of Pittsburgh, School of Education, December 1965.

Blacher-Dixon, J. *Preschool for the gifted-handicapped: Is it untimely, or about time?* Paper presented at the 55th Annual International Convention of the Council for Exceptional Children, Atlanta, April 1977.

Bloom, B. (Ed.). *Taxonomy of educational objectives*. New York: McKay, 1969.

Boehm, A., & Weinberg, R. *The classroom observer: A guide for developing observation skills*. New York: Teachers College Press, 1977.

Bonsall, M. The temperament of gifted children. *California Journal of Educational Research*, 1955, *6*, 162–165.

Borland, J. Teacher identification of the gifted: A new look. *Journal for the Education of the Gifted*, 1978, *2*, 22–32.

Braga, J.L. Analysis and evaluation of early admission to school for mentally advanced children. *The Journal of Educational Research*, 1969, *63*, 103–106.

Braga, J.L. Early admission: Opinion vs. evidence. *The Elementary School Journal*, 1971, *72*, 35–46.

Braggett, E.J. *Summary of an investigation: The effect of preschool kindergarten attendance on the cognitive development of children of above-average intelligence*. Newcastle, Australia: Department of Education, University of Newcastle, 1975. (ERIC ED 113057)

Bruch, C.B. Modification of procedures for identification of the disadvantaged gifted. *The Gifted Child Quarterly*, 1971, *15*, 267-272.

Bruner, J., Olver, R., & Greenfield, P.M. *Studies in cognitive growth*. New York: Wiley, 1966.

Burks, B.S., Jensen, D.W., & Terman, L.M. *Genetic studies of genius: The promise of youth: Follow-up studies of a thousand gifted children*. Stanford, CA: Stanford University Press, 1930.

Buros, O.K. (Ed.). *The seventh mental measurements yearbook* (Vol. 1). Edison, NJ: The Gryphon Press, 1972; *The eighth mental measurements yearbook*, 1978.

Buss, A.H., & Plomin, R. *A temperament theory of personality development*. New York: Wiley, 1975.

Cattell, J.M. Families of American men of science. *The Popular Science Monthly*, 1915, *86*, 504-515.

Chen, J., & Goon, S.W. Recognition of the gifted from among disadvantaged Asian children. *The Gifted Child Quarterly*, 1976, *20*, 157-164.

Chess, S. Temperament and learning ability of school children. *American Journal of Public Health*, 1968, *58*, 2231-2239.

Chess, S., Thomas, A., & Cameron, M. Temperament: Its significance for early schooling. *New York University Educational Quarterly*, 1976, *7*, 24-29.

Cheyney, A.B. Parents view their intellectually gifted children. *Peabody Journal of Education*, 1962, *40*, 98-101.

Child Development Institute. Gifted-Handicapped Project taps talents. *Developments from the Child Development Institute of the University of North Carolina at Chapel Hill*, 1977, *4*(2), 2-3.

Child Development Research Group. *Preschool evaluation report*. Draft for U.S. Office of Education. Seattle: University of Washington, 1978.

Christensen, E. Personal communication, March 1978.

Ciha, T.E., Harris, T.E., Hoffman, C., & Potter, M.W. Parents as identifiers of giftedness, ignored but accurate. *The Gifted Child Quarterly*, 1974, *18*, 191-195.

Coates, S., & Bromberg, P.M. Factorial structure of the Wechsler Preschool and Primary Scale of Intelligence between the ages of 4 and 6½. *Journal of Consulting and Clinical Psychology*, 1973, *40*, 364-370.

Coie, J.D., & Dorval, B. Sex differences in the intellectual structure of social interaction skills. *Developmental Psychology*, 1973, *8*, 261-267.

Comba, T. Personal communication, April 1978.

Combs, M.L., & Slaby, D.A. Social skills training with children. In B. Lahey & A. Kazdin (Eds.), *Advances in clinical psychology* (Vol. 1). New York: Plenum Press, 1978.

Connolly, A.J., Nachtman, W., & Pritchett, E.M. *KeyMath Diagnostic Arithmetic Test manual*. Circle Pines, MN: American Guidance Service, 1976.

Cornish, R.C. Parents', teachers', and pupils' perception of the gifted child's ability. *The Gifted Child Quarterly*, 1968, *12*, 14-17.

Cox, C.M. *Genetic studies of genius: The early mental traits of three hundred geniuses* (Vol. 2). Stanford, CA: Stanford University Press, 1926.

Cox, J.A. Suggested instruments for the identification of the preschool and kindergarten disadvantaged gifted. *Southern Journal of Educational Research,* 1974, *8* (5), 198–208.

Crockenberg, S.B. Creativity tests: A boon or boondoggle for education. *Review of Educational Research,* 1972, *42,* 27–45.

Daurio, S.P. *Educational enrichment versus acceleration: A review of the literature.* Unpublished manuscript, Department of Psychology, Johns Hopkins University, 1977.

Davidson, H.H. *Personality and economic background: A study of highly intelligent children.* New York: King's Crown Press, 1943.

Dunn, L.M. *Expanded manual for the Peabody Picture Vocabulary Test.* Circle Pines, MN: American Guidance Service, 1970.

Dunn, L.M., & Markwardt, F.C. *Manual for the Peabody Individual Achievement Test.* Circle Pines, MN: American Guidance Service, 1970.

Durkin, D. Children who learned to read at home. *Elementary School Journal,* 1961, *62,* 14–18.

Durkin, D. *Children who read early.* New York: Teachers College Press, 1966.

Ehrlich, V.Z. A model program for educating gifted 4-8 year-old children. *International Journal of Early Childhood Education,* in press.

Eliot, J., & Salkind, N.J. (Eds.). *Children's spatial development.* Springfield, IL: Charles C. Thomas, 1975.

Fortna, R.O., & Boston, B.O. *Testing the gifted child: An interpretation in lay language.* Reston, VA: The Council for Exceptional Children, 1976.

Fox, L.H. Programs for the gifted and talented: An overview. In A.H. Passow (Ed.), *The gifted and the talented: Their education and development.* The 78th Yearbook of the National Society on the Study of Education. Chicago: University of Chicago Press, 1979.

Frierson, E.C. Upper and lower status gifted children: A study of differences. *Exceptional Children,* 1965, *32,* 83–90.

Furth, H.G. *Piaget for teachers.* Englewood Cliffs, NJ: Prentice-Hall, 1970.

Gallagher, J.J. Peer acceptance of highly gifted children in elementary school. *Elementary School Journal,* 1958a, *58,* 465–470.

Gallagher, J.J. Social status of children related to intelligence, propinquity, and social perception. *Elementary School Journal,* 1958b, *58,* 225–231.

Gallagher, J.J. *Teaching the gifted child.* Boston: Allyn & Bacon, 1975.

Gallagher, J.J., & Crowder, T. The adjustment of gifted children in the regular classroom. *Exceptional Children,* 1957, *23,* 306–312, 317–319.

Gear, G.H. Effects of training on teachers' accuracy in the identification of gifted children. *The Gifted Child Quarterly,* 1978, *22*(1), 90–97.

Getzels, W., & Dillon, J.T. The nature of giftedness and the education of the gifted child. In R.W.M. Travers (Ed.), *Second handbook of research on teaching.* Chicago: Rand McNally, 1973.

Getzels, J.W., & Jackson, P.W. *Creativity and intelligence: Explorations with gifted students.* New York: Wiley, 1962.

Ginsburg, H. *The myth of the deprived child.* Englewood Cliffs, NJ: Prentice-Hall, 1972.

Goldschmidt, M., & Bentler, F. *Concept Assessment Kit.* San Diego: Educational and Industrial Testing Service, 1968.

Gordon, E.M., & Thomas, A. Children's behavioral style and the teacher's appraisal of their intelligence. *Journal of School Psychology*, 1967, *5*, 292–300.

Gordon, I.J. An instructional theory approach to the analysis of selected early childhood programs. In I.J. Gordon (Ed.), *Early childhood education*. Seventy-first yearbook of the National Society for the Study of Education. Chicago: University of Chicago Press, 1972.

Gorsuch, R.L., Henighan, R.P., & Barnard, C. Locus of control: An example of dangers in using children's scales with children. *Child Development*, 1972, *43*, 579–590.

Groth, N. Mothers of gifted. *The Gifted Child Quarterly*, 1975, *19*, 217–222.

Guilford, J.R. *The nature of human intelligence*. New York: McGraw-Hill, 1967.

Hall, A.S., & Roedell, W.C. *Programs for intellectually advanced preschool children: Developing social skills*. Unpublished manuscript, University of Washington, Child Development Research Group, 1978.

Hall, J.C., & Chansky, N.M. Relationships between selected ability and achievement tests in an economically disadvantaged Negro sample. *Psychological Reports*, 1971, *28*, 741–742.

Hanninen, G. Personal communication, April 1978.

Hartup, W.W. Peer interaction and social organization. In P.H. Mussen (Ed.), *Carmichael's manual of child psychology* (Vol. 2). New York: Wiley, 1970.

Hauck, B.B., & Freehill, M.F. *The gifted—case studies*. Dubuque, IA: William C. Brown, 1972.

Heber, R.F. The relation of intelligence and physical maturity to social status of children. *Journal of Educational Psychology*, 1956, *47*, 158–162.

Hildreth, G. Characteristics of young gifted children. *The Journal of Genetic Psychology*, 1938, *53*, 287–311.

Hildreth, G. Three gifted children: A developmental study. *The Journal of Genetic Psychology*, 1954, *85*, 239–262.

Hitchfield, E.M. *In search of promise*. London: Longman Group Ltd., 1973.

Hobson, J.R. Mental age as a workable criterion for school admission. *Elementary School Journal*, 1948, *48*, 312–321.

Hokanson, D.T., & Jospe, M. *The search for cognitive giftedness in exceptional children*. Unpublished report. New Haven, CT: Educational Center for the Arts, 1976.

Hollingworth, L.S. *Children above 180 IQ*. New York: World Book Company, 1942.

Horn, J.L. Human abilities: A review of research and theory in the early 1970's. In M.R. Rosenzweig & L.W. Porter (Ed.), *Annual review of psychology* (Vol. 27). Palo Alto: Annual Reviews, Inc., 1976.

Hubbard, R. A method of studying spontaneous group formation. In D. Thomas & Associates, *Some new techniques for studying social behavior* (Chap. IV). New York: Child Development Monographs 1, Bureau of Publications, Teachers College, Columbia University, 1929.

Humes, C.W., Jr., & Eberhardt, D.G. The multi-level approach to the identification of kindergarten gifted pupils. *North Carolina Association for the Gifted and Talented Quarterly Journal*, 1977, *3*(1), 10–16.

Hunt, J. McV. *Intelligence and experience*. New York: Ronald Press, 1961.

Irwin, D.M., & Ambron, S.R. *Moral judgment and role-taking in children ages three to seven*.

Paper presented at the meeting of the Society for Research in Child Development, Philadelphia, 1973.

Jackson, N.E. Identification and description of intellectual precocity in young children. In H.B. Robinson (Chair), *Intellectually advanced children: Preliminary findings of a longitudinal study.* Symposium presented at the Annual Convention of the American Psychological Association, Toronto, August 30, 1978a.

Jackson, N.E. *Passing the individual differences test: A cram course for developmental psychologists.* Seattle: University of Washington, Child Development Research Group, 1979. (ERIC ED 174358)

Jackson, N.E., & Robinson, H.B. Early identification of intellectually advanced children. In Robinson et al., *Identification and nurturance of extraordinarily precocious young children: Annual report to the Spencer Foundation.* Seattle: University of Washington, Child Development Research Group, 1977. (ERIC ED 151095)

Jackson, N.E., Robinson, H.B., & Dale, P.S. *Cognitive development in young children.* Monterey, CA: Brooks/Cole, 1977.

Jacobs, J.C. Effectiveness of teacher and parent identification of gifted children as a function of school level. *Psychology in the Schools, 1971, 8,* 140–142.

Jenkins, M.D. Case studies of Negro children of Binet IQ 160 and above. *Journal of Negro Education,* 1943, *12,* 159–166.

Jensen, A.R. How much can we boost I.Q. and scholastic achievement? *Harvard Educational Review,* 1969, *39,* 1–23.

Kamii, C.K., & Radin, N.L. A framework for a preschool curriculum based on some Piagetian concepts. *Journal of Creative Behavior,* 1967, *1,* 314–326.

Kamin, L. J. *The science and politics of IQ.* Potomac, MD: Lawrence Erlbaum Associates, 1974.

Kaplan, D. Personal communication, April 1978.

Kaplan, S. *Providing programs for the gifted and talented: A handbook.* Reston, VA: The Council for Exceptional Children, 1975.

Karnes, M.B. *Program performance report for handicapped children's early education program,* Part I (Grant #GOO-75-00232). Washington, D.C.: Department of Health, Education and Welfare, Bureau of Education for the Handicapped, 1977.

Karnes, M.B., & Bertschi, J.D. Identifying and educating gifted/talented nonhandicapped and handicapped preschoolers. *Teaching Exceptional Children,* 1978, *10,* 114–119.

Karnes, M.B., Teska, J.A., & Hodgins, A.S. The successful implementation of a highly specific preschool instructional program by paraprofessional teachers. *The Journal of Special Education,* 1970, *4*(1), 69–80.

Kaufman, A.S. Comparison of the WPPSI, Stanford-Binet, and McCarthy Scales as predictors of first-grade achievement. *Perceptual and Motor Skills,* 1973a, *36,* 67–73.

Kaufman, A.S. Analysis of the McCarthy Scales in terms of Guilford's structure of intellect model. *Perceptual and Motor Skills,* 1973b, *36,* 967–976.

Kaufman, A.S., & Hollenbeck, G.P. Factor analysis of the standardization edition of the McCarthy Scales. *Journal of Clinical Psychology,* 1973, *29,* 359–362.

Kincaid, D. A study of highly gifted elementary pupils. *The Gifted Child Quarterly,* 1969, *13,* 264–267.

Klausmeier, H.J. Physical, behavioral and other characteristics of high- and lower-achieving children in favored environments. *Journal of Educational Research*, 1958, *51*, 573–581.

Krinsky, R. *Use of parent information in the screening of precocious intellectual development in young children.* Unpublished manuscript, University of Washington, Child Development Research Group, 1978.

Krinsky, R., Jackson, N.E., & Robinson, H.B. Analysis of parent information in the identification of precocious intellectual development in young children. In H.B. Robinson, et al., *Identification and nurturance of extraordinarily precocious young children: Annual report to the Spencer Foundation.* Seattle: University of Washington, Child Development Research Group, 1977. (ERIC ED 151 095).

Krinsky, S.G., Sjursen, F., Krinsky, R., Jackson, N.E., & Robinson, H.B. *Conservation in intellectually advanced children of preschool age: Levels of performance and relation to other intellectual and academic abilities.* Unpublished manuscript, University of Washington, Child Development Research Group, 1977.

Laycock, F., & Caylor, J.S. Physiques of gifted children and their less gifted siblings. *Child Development*, 1964, *35*, 63–74.

Lazar, L., Hubbell, V., Murray, H., Rosche, M., & Royce, J. *Summary report: The persistence of preschool effects.* Summary of final report to the Administration of Children, Youth, and Families, Department of Health, Education, and Welfare, October 1977.

Lehman, H.C. *Age and achievement.* Princeton: Princeton University Press: 1953.

Leithwood, K.A. Motor, cognitive and affective relationships among advantaged preschool children. *Research Quarterly*, 1971, *42*, 47–53.

Levine, S., Elzey, F.F., & Lewis, M. *California preschool social competency scale.* Palo Alto, CA: Consulting Psychologist Press, Inc., 1969.

Liddle, G. Overlap among desirable and undesirable characteristics in gifted children. *Journal of Educational Psychology*, 1958, *49*, 219–223.

Livesley, W.J., & Bromley, D.B. *Person perception in childhood and adolescence.* London: Wiley, 1973.

Lovell, K., & Shields, J.B. Some aspects of a study of the gifted child. *British Journal of Educational Psychology*, 1967, *37*, 201–208.

Maccoby, E.E., & Jacklin, C.N. *The psychology of sex differences.* Stanford: CA: Stanford University Press, 1974.

Macey, T. *The use of temperament characteristics for describing and identifying children with advanced mental abilities.* Unpublished Master's thesis, University of Washington, School of Social Work, 1978.

Malone, C.E. *Parent inventory—kindergarten.* San Diego, CA: Western Behavioral Sciences Institute, 1975/76.

Malone, C.E., & Moonan, W.J. Behavioral identification of gifted children. *The Gifted Child Quarterly*, 1975, *19*, 301–306.

Mancini, P. School for whiz kids. *New York*, November 14, 1977, 73–87.

Mann, H. How real are friendships of gifted and typical children in a program of partial segregation? *Exceptional Children*, 1957, *23*, 199–201.

McCall, R.B., Hogarty, P.S., & Hurlburt, N. Transitions in infant sensorimotor development and the prediction of childhood IQ, *American Psychologist*, 1972, 27, 728–748.

McCarthy, D. *Manual for the McCarthy Scales of Children's Abilities.* New York: Psychological Corporation, 1972.

McClelland, S. *The reading recognition quick check.* Unpublished assessment tool, University of Washington, Child Development Research Group, 1977a.

McClelland, S. *Creativity and intellectually advanced preschoolers: A preliminary investigation.* Unpublished manuscript, University of Washington, Child Development Research Group, 1977b.

McCurdy, H. The childhood pattern of genius. *Journal of the Elisha Mitchell Scientific Society*, 1957, 448–462.

McNemar, Q. *The revision of the Stanford-Binet Scale.* Boston: Houghton Mifflin, 1942.

Meeker, M. *The structure of intellect: Its interpretation and uses.* Columbus, OH: Charles E. Merrill, 1969.

Mensh, I. Rorschach study of the gifted child: A survey of the literature. *Exceptional Children*, 1950, pp. 8–14, 17–18.

Meyers, C. E., Orpet, R.E., Atwell, A.A., & Dingman, H.F. Primary abilities at mental age six. *Monographs of the Society for Research in Child Development*, 1962, 27.

Miller, B. Personal communication, April 1978.

Miller, J., Roedell, W.C., Slaby, R., & Robinson, H.B. *Sex-role development in intellectually precocious preschool children.* Paper presented at the meeting of the Western Psychological Association, San Francisco, April 1978.

Miller, R.V. Social status and socioempathic differences among mentally superior, mentally typical, and mentally retarded children. *Exceptional Children*, 1956, 23, 114–119.

Newland, T.E. *The gifted in socio-educational perspective.* Englewood Cliffs, NJ: Prentice-Hall, 1976.

Oden, M. The fulfillment of promise: Forty-year follow-up of the Terman gifted group. *Genetic Psychology Monographs*, 1968, 27, 3–93.

Ogilvie, E. *Gifted children in primary schools.* London: Macmillan Education Ltd., 1973.

O'Shea, H. Friendship and the intellectually gifted child. *Exceptional Children*, 1960, 26, 327–335.

Parkyn, G.W. *Children of high intelligence.* New York: Oxford University Press, 1948.

Paschal, E. *Encouraging the excellent.* New York: The Fund for the Advancement of Education, 1960.

Pegnato, C.W., & Birch, J.W. Locating gifted children in junior high schools—a comparison of methods. *Exceptional Children*, 1959, 25, 300–304.

Pennsylvania Department of Education. *Mentally gifted children and youth: A guide for parents.* Harrisburg: Bureau of Special and Compensatory Education, 1973.

Piaget, J. *Psychology of intelligence.* Totowa, NJ: Littlefield-Adams, 1966.

Piaget, J. *Science of education and the psychology of the child.* New York: Viking Press, 1971.

Plessas, G.P., & Oakes, C.R. Prereading experiences of selected early readers. *The Reading Teacher*, 1964, 17, 241–245.

Pringle, M.L.K. *Able misfits.* London: Longman, 1970.

Ramsey, P.H., & Vane, J.R. A factor-analytic study of the Stanford-Binet with young children. *Journal of School Psychology*, 1970, *8*, 278–284.

Raven, J.C., Court, J.H., & Raven, J. *Manual for Raven's progressive matrices and vocabulary scales*. London: H.K. Lewis & Co., Lts., 1976.

Rellas, A. The use of the Wechsler Preschool and Primary Scale (WPPSI) in the early identification of gifted students. *California Journal of Educational Research*, 1969, *20*, 117–119.

Renzulli, J.S. Talent potential in minority group students. *Exceptional Children*, 1973, *39*, 437–444.

Renzulli, J.S., & Hartman, R.K. Scale for rating behavioral characteristics of superior students. *Exceptional Children*, 1971, *38*, 243–247.

Renzulli, J.S., Hartman, R.K., & Callahan, C.M. Teacher identification of superior students. *Exceptional Children*, 1971, *38*, 211–214.

Renzulli, J.S., & Smith, L. Two approaches to identification of gifted students. *Exceptional Children*, 1971, *38*, 211–214.

Research Report. Can preschool education make a lasting difference? *Bulletin of the High Scope Foundation*, 1977, *4*, 1–8.

Reynolds, M.C. (Ed.). *Early school admission for mentally advanced children*. Washington, D.C.: The Council for Exceptional Children, 1962.

Risley, T.R., & Baer, D.M. Operant behavior modification: The deliberate development of behavior. In B.M. Caldwell & H.N. Ricciuti (Eds.), *Review of child development research* (Vol. 3). Chicago: University of Chicago Press, 1973.

Robinson, H.B. Current myths concerning gifted children. National/State Leadership Training Institute, Gifted and Talented Brief No. 5, October 1977, 1–11.

Robinson, H.B., Jackson, N.E., & Roedell, W.C. *Annual report to the Spencer Foundation: Identification and nurturance of extraordinarily precocious young children*. Seattle: University of Washington, Child Development Research Group, 1978. (ERIC ED 162 756)

Robinson, H.B., Jackson, N.E., & Roedell, W.C. *Annual report to the Spencer Foundation: Identification and nurturance of extraordinarily precocious young children*. Seattle: University of Washington, Child Development Research Group, 1978. (ERIC Document Reproduction Service No. pending)

Robinson, H.B., Roedell, W.C., & Jackson, N.E. Early identification and intervention. In A.H. Passow (Ed.), *The gifted and the talented: Their education and development*. The 78th yearbook of the National Society for the Study of Education. Chicago: University of Chicago Press, 1979.

Roedell, W.C. Individual differences among intellectually advanced children. In T. Naumann (Chair), *Current research concerning gifted young children*. Symposium presented at the Annual Meeting of the Western Psychological Association, Seattle, April 21, 1977a.

Roedell, W.C. Issues in the assessment of social-emotional development. In H.B. Robinson (Chair), *Assessment of advanced intellectual abilities in young children*. Symposium presented at the Fifth Annual Pacific Northwest Research and Evaluation Conference, Seattle, May 27, 1977b.

Roedell, W.C. Social development in intellectually advanced children. In H.B. Robinson (Chair), *Intellectually advanced children: Preliminary findings of a longitudinal study.* Symposium presented at the Annual Convention of the American Psychological Association, Toronto, August 30, 1978.

Roedell, W.C., & Robinson, H.B. *Programming for intellectually advanced children: A program development guide.* Seattle: University of Washington, Child Development Research Group, 1977. (ERIC ED 151 094)

Roedell, W.C., Slaby, R.G., & Robinson, H.B. *Social development in young children.* Monterey, CA: Brooks/Cole, 1977.

Roeper, A. Gifted preschooler and the Montessori method. *The Gifted Child Quarterly,* 1966, *10,* 83–89.

Roeper, A. Finding the clue to children's thought processes. *Young Children,* 1966, *21,* 335–348.

Roeper, A. Personal communication, April 1978.

Rothenberg, B.B. Children's social sensitivity and the relationship to interpersonal competence, intrapersonal comfort, and intellectual level. *Developmental Psychology,* 1970, *2,* 335–350.

Rubin, K.H. Egocentrism in childhood: A unitary construct? *Child Development,* 1973, *44,* 102–110.

Ruschival, M.L., & Way, J.G. The WPPSI and the Stanford-Binet: A validity and reliability study using gifted preschool children. *Journal of Consulting and Clinical Psychology,* 1971, *37,* 163.

Ryan, J.S. *Early identification of intellectually superior black children.* Unpublished doctoral dissertation, University of Michigan, 1975.

Salvia, J., Ysseldyke, J.E., & Lee, M. 1972 revision of the Stanford-Binet: A farewell to the mental age. *Psychology in the Schools,* 1975, *12,* 421–422.

Sattler, J.M. *Assessment of children's intelligence.* Philadelphia: Saunders, 1974.

Schuster, P. *Learning and enrichment for able preschoolers.* Unpublished manuscript, Johns Hopkins University, 1976.

Seattle Public Schools. *Horizon parent questionnaire.* Seattle: February 1978.

Shantz, C.U. The development of social cognition. In E.M. Hetherington (Ed.), *Review of child development research* (Vol. 5). Chicago: University of Chicago Press, 1975.

Sheldon, P.M. The families of highly gifted children. *Marriage and Family Living,* 1954, *16,* 59–61.

Shorr, D.N. Personal communication, June 1978.

Shorr, D.N., Jackson, N.E., & Robinson, H.B. Achievement test performance of intellectually advanced preschool children. *Exceptional Children,* in press.

Shorr, D.N., & McClelland, S.E. Assessing general intellectual status in bright preschool children. In T. Naumann (Chair), *Current research concerning gifted young children.* Symposium presented at the Annual Meeting of the Western Psychological Association, Seattle, April 21, 1977.

Shorr, D.N., McClelland, S.E., & Robinson, H.B. Corrected mental age scores for the Stanford-Binet Intelligence Scale. *Measurement and Evaluation in Guidance,* 1977, *10,* 144–147.

Singer, D., & Rummo, J. Ideational creativity and behavioral style in kindergarten-age children. *Developmental Psychology,* 1973, *8*(2), 154–161.

Singer, D., & Whitton, M.B. Ideational creativity and expressive aspects of human figure drawing in kindergarten-age children. *Developmental Psychology*, 1971, 4(3), 366–369.

Sisk, D. From the classroom. *The Gifted Child Quarterly*, 1977, 21, 552–554.

Slaby, R., & Frey, F. Development of gender constancy and selection attention to same-sex models. *Child Development*, 1975, 46, 849–856.

Slosson, R.L. *Slosson Intelligence test (SIT) for Children and Adults*. New York: Slosson Educational Publications, 1963.

Sontag, L.W., Baker, C.T., & Nelson, V.L. Mental growth and personality development: A longitudinal study. *Monographs of the Society for Research in Child Development*, 1958, 23(2, Serial No. 68).

Spivack, G., & Shure, M.B. *Social adjustment of young children*. San Francisco: Jossey-Bass, 1974.

Standards for educational and psychological tests. Washington, D.C.: American Psychological Association, 1966, 1974.

Stanley, J.C. Rationale for the study of mathematically precocious youth. In J.C. Stanley, W.C. George, & C.H. Solano (Eds.), *The gifted and the creative: A fifty-year perspective*. Baltimore: Johns Hopkins University Press, 1977.

Starkweather, E.K. Problems in the measurement of creativity in preschool children. *Journal of Educational Measurement*, 1964, 1, 109–113.

Starkweather, E. Creativity research instruments designed for use with preschool children. *The Journal of Creative Behavior*, 1971, 5, 245–255.

Stevenson, H.W., Parker, T., Wilkinson, A., & Fish, E. Predictive value of teachers' ratings of young children. *Journal of Educational Psychology*, 1976, 68, 507–517.

Stutsman, R. Guide for administering the Merrill-Palmer Scale of Mental Tests. In L.M. Terman (Ed.), *Measurement and adjustment series (Part III). Mental measurement of preschool children*. New York: Harcourt Brace, 1931 and 1949.

Sutherland, A., & Goldschmidt, M.L. Negative teacher expectation and change in children with superior intellectual potential. *Child Development*, 1974, 45, 852–856.

Terman, L.M. *Genetic studies of genius: Mental and physical traits of a thousand gifted children* (Vol. 1). Stanford, CA: Stanford University Press, 1925.

Terman, L.M., & Merrill, M.A. *Stanford-Binet Intelligence Scale manual for the third revision, form L-M*. Boston: Houghton Mifflin, 1973.

Terman, L.M., & Oden, M.H. *Genetic studies of genius: The gifted child grows up: Twenty-five years' follow-up of a superior group* (Vol. 4). Stanford, CA: Stanford University Press, 1947.

Terman, M., & Oden, M.N. *Genetic studies of genius. The gifted group at mid-life: Thirty-five years' follow-up of the superior child* (Vol. 5). Stanford, CA: Stanford University Press, 1959.

Thomas, A., & Chess, S. Behavioral individuality in childhood. In L.R. Aronson, E. Tobach, D.S. Lehrman, & J.S. Rosenblatt (Eds.), *Development and evolution of behavior*. San Francisco: Freeman, 1970.

Thomas, A., & Chess, S. *Temperament and development*. New York: Brunner/Mazel, 1977.

Thomas, A., Chess, S., Birch, H.G., Hertzig, M., & Korn, S. *Behavioral individuality in early childhood.* New York: New York University Press, 1963.

Thompson, W.R., & Grusec, J. Studies of early experience. In P.H. Mussen (Ed.), *Carmichael's manual of child psychology* (Vol. 1). New York: Wiley, 1970.

Thorndike, E.L. Intelligence and its measurement. *Journal of Educational Psychology,* 1921, *12,* 124–127.

Thorndike, R.L. Review of the Torrance Tests of Creative Thinking. In D.K. Buros (Ed.), *The seventh mental measurements yearbook* (Vol. 1). Edison, NJ: The Gryphon Press, 1972.

Tittle, B. Personal communication, April 1978.

Torrance, E.P. *Education and the creative potential.* Minneapolis: University of Minnesota Press, 1963.

Torrance, E.P. *Torrance Tests for Creative Thinking: gr. K-graduate school* (Red. ed.) Los Angeles: Western Psychological Services, 1966–1974.

Torrance, E.P. Are the Torrance Tests of Creative Thinking biased against or in favor of "disadvantaged" groups? *The Gifted Child Quarterly,* 1971, *15,* 75–80.

Torrance, E.P. *Thinking creatively in action and movement* (Research Ed.) Athens: University of Georgia, Georgia Studies of Creative Behavior, 1974.

Torrey, J.W. Learning to read without a teacher: A case study. *Elementary English,* 1969, *46,* 550–556.

U.S. Office of Education. *Education of the gifted and talented.* Washington, D.C.: U.S. Government Printing Office, 1972.

U.S. Office of Education. Undiscovered and undeveloped talent. *School and Society,* 1972, *100,* 210.

Walker, D.K. *Socioemotional measures for preschool and kindergarten children.* San Francisco: Jossey-Bass, 1973.

Walker, D.K., Bane, M.J., & Bryk, A. *The quality of the Head Start planned variation data.* Cambridge, Mass.: Huron Institute, 1973.

Wallach, M.A. Creativity. In P.H. Mussen (Ed.), *Carmichael's manual of child psychology* (Vol. 1). New York: Wiley, 1970.

Wallach, M.A., & Kogan, N. *Modes of thinking in young children.* New York: Holt, 1965.

Ward, W. Creativity and environmental cues in nursery school children. *Developmental Psychology,* 1969, *1,* 543–547.

Ward, W.C. The Make-A-Tree Test. In S.B. Anderson et al., *CIRCUS manual and technical report.* Princeton, NJ: Educational Testing Service, 1974–75, 1979.

Wechsler, D. *Manual for the Preschool and Primary Scale of Intelligence.* New York: Psychological Corporation, 1967.

Wechsler, D. *Manual for the Wechsler Intelligence Scale for Children-Revised.* New York: Psychological Corporation, 1974.

Weikart, D.P., McClelland, D., Smith, S.A., Klug, J., Judson, A., & Taylor, C. *The cognitive curriculum.* Ypsilanti, Mich.: High Scope Educational Research Foundation, 1970.

Weikart, D.P., Rogers, L., & Adcock, C. *The cognitively oriented curriculum.* Urbana: University of Illinois, 1971.

Weise, P., Meyers, C.E., & Tuel, J.K. PMA factors, sex and teacher nomination in screening kindergarten gifted. *Educational and Psychological Measurement,* 1965, *25,* 597-603.

Willerman, L., & Fiedler, M.F. Intellectually precocious preschool children: Early development and later intellectual accomplishments. *Journal of Genetic Psychology,* 1977, *131,* 13-20.

Williams, F.E. *Classroom ideas for encouraging thinking and feeling.* Buffalo, N.Y.: D.O.K. Publishers, 1970.

Williams, J.D., Teubner, J., & Harlow, S.D. Creativity in rural, urban and Indian children. *The Journal of Psychology,* 1973, *83,* 111-116.

Witty, P., & Coomer, A. A case study of gifted twin boys. *Exceptional Children,* 1955, *22,* 104-108.

INDEX